T0197226

MY CANCER LIFE!
NOT DEATH

Joseph Hodge

WestBow Press books may be ordered through booksellers or by contacting:

WestBow Press
A Division of Thomas Nelson & Zondervan
1663 Liberty Drive
Bloomington, IN 47403
www.westbowpress.com
1 (866) 928-1240

ISBN: 978-1-9736-6533-5 (sc)
ISBN: 978-1-9736-6534-2 (e)

Library of Congress Control Number: 2019907264

Print information available on the last page.

WestBow Press rev. date: 06/13/2019

For my wife, Michelle, and children, Mykal, Marea, and Mathue. Also to my wonderful son-in-law, Corey, and daughter-in-law, Victoria, and to Christina. For my outstanding God-given physician, Dr. Andrew Parchman, and the dedicated, wonderful nurses and staff of TriHealth Cancer Institute.

Foreword

I have had the privilege of taking care of Joe for nearly four years now. I have been part of his trials and tribulations during that time period. As a nurse, being able to experience the best of times and the worst of times with patients is something that we hold near and dear to our hearts. Experiencing times like that together truly makes you value your professional relationship as a friendship, and when they hurt, you hurt; when they smile, you smile. Joseph has taken his journey from one of despair to one of hope. It is an inspiration to watch someone truly learn from such a defeating situation and turn it into an experience that he wants to share with the world, offering hope to others who may be experiencing something similar. It has been my pleasure to play a role in Joseph's care and get to know him over the years.

—Kim B., RN, OCN

Acknowledgments

Special thanks to God for His divine inspiration and to my wife, Michelle, of thirty-eight years, who stood by my side throughout this whole illness and book process and kept me encouraged. She read every sentence, critiqued every page, and worked tirelessly after her own job to help me get this completed.

I want to give thanks to my family, who watched me through my struggles day by day and gave me encouragement to not give up.

Finally, I also want to give thanks to the wonderful staff of the TriHealth Cancer Institute who read the beginning of this book and encouraged me to continue and finish and publish it.

Preface

Sitting in the Cancer Center, I decided to write a letter to my children about what I was going through so that they would not fall into the depression that is common in people who have a loved one who has been diagnosed with cancer. Little did I know it would blossom into this book.

I need them to stand up and be the men and women they are and not change with every tumultuous wind that blows into their lives, foolishly blaming God for any unpleasant circumstance that comes.

Hopefully this book will inspire and help people to see that even though some cancers are a means to an end, cancer is only one small part of life. Eventually, all bodies will return to the earth by one method or another.

So, with this in mind, is cancer a death sentence or is it an early warning (grace period) to get things right and shower family and friends with extraordinary love?

So what's the correct response when the doctor says, "Stage 4 prostate cancer with bone mets"? This means an average of two years of life remaining. Now that was a fun-filled appointment! This news came two weeks before Thanksgiving and just weeks before Christmas. This time of year, most people get a turkey dinner and presents. Me, I got three weeks of hospital food and lots of extreme pain. This pain resulted in a weight loss of one hundred pounds in three weeks.

A lot to hold on to at once, huh? I didn't know what to think or how to process thoughts in this period of my life. I was very religious but not exactly what you would call holy. This experience was about to teach me the difference.

My first lesson was that of the fig tree (Mark 11:13–10). It's not so hard to make a good showing when living up to people's standards. That's the problem. People are easily pleased by good works. God expects fruit from every life. That tree looked like it had fruit, but it didn't. Thanks be to God that we are more to him than trees, so we get a warning.

It was time to actually produce the fruit that was required of my tree. At this point in my life, God is looking for the fruit he planted in me that can only come forth in spirit form.

I was in my early fifties, having a serious midlife crisis. In my mind, this is where an old man seeks the attention of a younger woman. However, in God's eyes, this is different. Most of my life, I catered only to my human senses, not realizing that flesh is only one phase of life.

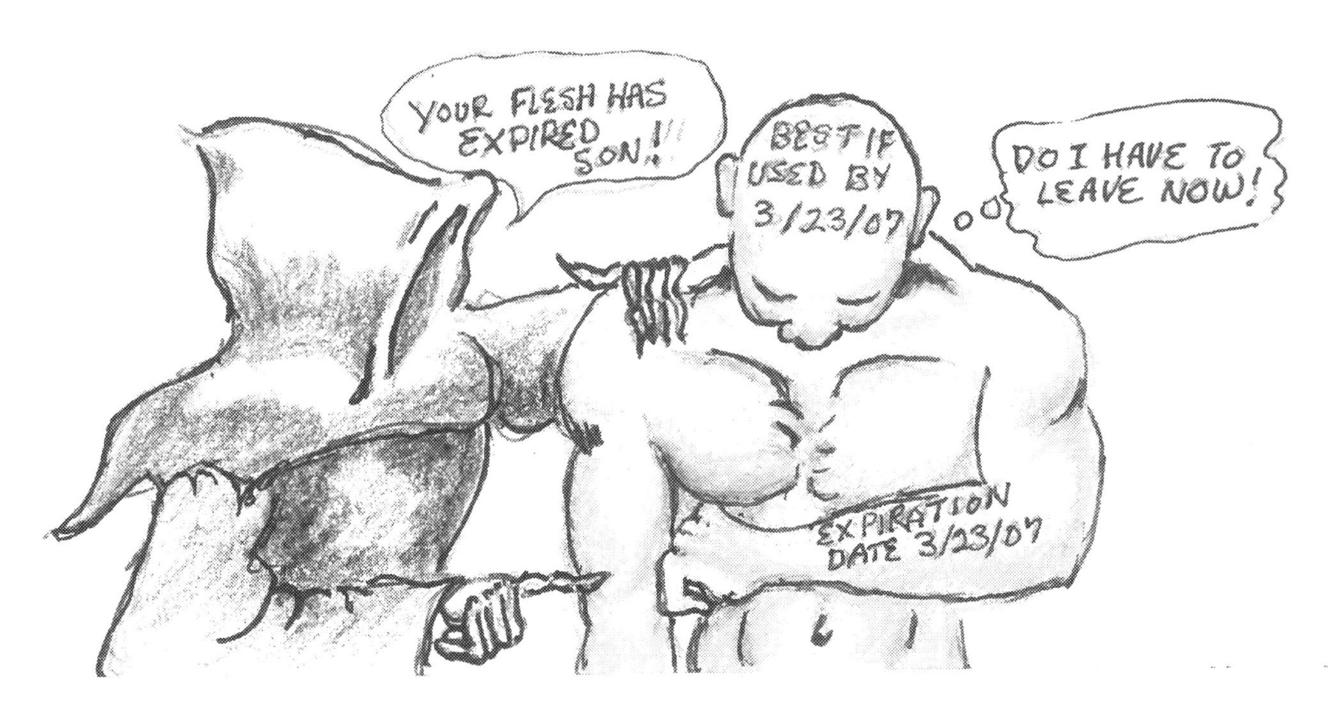

It's like an eviction notice. You have only so many days to pack up and leave. A smart person will inventory their stuff to see what they should keep, give away, sell, or store. In life, we are supposed to give a lot more than we do. This is God's design for a very selfish world. Funny how pain and suffering with an added death sentence tends to strip away all the unnecessities of life.

Back to the midlife crisis. A midlife crisis is when a person gets through over half of their life and hasn't made any preparation for the latter half. At fifty, and doing fine in pretty much every aspect of natural life, I was not prepared for the approaching transformation from natural life to spiritual life. The world's definition of life is work, pleasure, and some sort of church service on Sunday.

This sort of living makes God, who is the very breath of life, very small in the scheme of life itself. Just because you can't see the ocean from Ohio doesn't mean it's not there. I realized that all I had ever learned of God in my fifty-plus years was simply an introduction to God. Just because I have the Holy Ghost doesn't mean I have figured out God. Paul said, "To be absent in flesh is to be present with the Lord" (2 Cor. 5:8). This I know to be true.

Lying in a hospital bed with the life draining out of you is a two-way street: one way bad, the other way good. Does my bucket list include preparation for eternal life, or is it squeezing the last bit of pleasure out of this life?

I've been told that I was a decent man, but many decent men have died without a personal walk with God. Sounds a bit unimportant, but God said, "I am God and I change not" (Mal. 3:6). He walked with humankind in the beginning, and he intends to walk with humankind now (Gen. 3:8). "Can two walk together except they be agreed" (Amos 3:3). Is my life agreeable to God?

I'm definitely mortal. Now I know I don't even have the power to wake up tomorrow. No medical magic tricks to keep me alive. Grace and mercy are my closest friends. In the hospital, my life went into a free fall toward death. I and everyone I love were powerless to do anything to help me. The Bible calls this experience a Euroclydon. You can say you don't believe in the Bible, but in the end, you will find the beginning, middle, and end of every person's life.

Anyway, in this situation, Paul ends up on a ship in the middle of one of life's terrible, life-threatening storms (we all have them). Some storms people don't know the meaning of, so they end up drowning in sorrow or deep depression. Hopelessness is when you don't have God's Word to hold your soul together. At this point, where flesh and spirit are beginning to separate (and they will), you need a connection with God (the Spirit), who brings you into the next phase of life. I lay in the hospital bed all drugged up with the strongest drugs available. My body was shutting down, but my Spirit man was more active than my body ever was.

Let me explain, going back to Paul in the storm. This ship was like my body that was strong until the storm hit. It was overwhelmed by wave after wave of pain. Pain corrodes the human mind when it's uncontrolled, much like that storm Paul was in when the waves ripped apart that ship (Acts 27:14–44). I'm overjoyed because God blessed me to remember His Word that was taught to me throughout my self-centered life. After the ship —my body and my life—was all but destroyed (like the ship that Paul was on), God allowed my tortured mind to retain enough of His Word to have something to hold on to in the Euroclydon (which is not your average rainstorm).

In this shipwreck called cancer, I have to find my way back to land. In the mind of humans, this is sanity. Just like the people on that ship, your mind goes to work checking every lifeboat that is available. After much consideration, (like God revealed to Paul) if the ship can't handle the storm, you don't have a chance in a little lifeboat. Obviously, a storm of this magnitude will reduce a lifeboat to splinters.

Even in this temporary life, there are external benefits that we can obtain that benefit us in this phase of life and the next. The professional sailors on the boat were experts at sailing with a whole ship, but what happens when you must navigate the seas of life with a wounded or broken ship? All the rules change. Paul was not a sailor, but no doubt he had heard shipwreck stories in his life. Now that he himself was involved in a shipwreck, his reality or perspective on life changed drastically. In this place in life, any solution seems reasonable. It is this perspective that makes you want to get off of a ship and into a small, wooden lifeboat in the middle of a raging storm. In other words, doubt God's Word (that is settled in heaven and unchangeable) for a bottle of pain pills. If you noticed, the lifeboat was never mentioned again, as it most likely disappeared under the stormy seas.

Any situation, good or bad, is always better when you are anchored in faith. Paul lets us know that in God's Word there is salvation for everyone. Some people grabbed part of the ship. Those who didn't have that option were still saved. God allowed them to use their skill of swimming to swim to safety. Death had not one victory!

Saved, yes, but there are two other characters humankind must deal with (with God or without God). These are hell and the grave. You and I will surely face them before it's all over. Hell, from my perspective, is your flesh failing you, and your soul is so far away from its maker (God) that it's constantly in want. For example (Luke 16:19–31), the rich man ended up in hell because he didn't drink of the everlasting water in his natural life. He was not able to access the benefit in his spiritual end, leaving him in want and without the presence of God (who is life) (John 4:10).

The Word of God is written solely for the good of humankind. You have to remember, knowledge was sidetracked in the Garden of Eden with the introduction of self-consciousness, moving humankind further away from God consciousness (we are made in His image). This brought out more animal instinct than human, with Cain killing his own brother. Clearly not God's plan for humankind. So God blessed us with His Word as a guide to those who still want to be godly—understanding it still takes a walk with God. It's very clear that God's Word is spiritual. To understand it, you must seek a spiritual mind. God's Word is the knowledge that is required at your transformation from this fleshly phase of life to your spiritual phase that is eternity. Satan would have us think that all of the education we need is in a schoolroom or a college. This will not work for you in transforming from natural life to spiritual life.

Getting back to the storms of life, now we have to deal with death. Death was present and accounted for once Paul escaped death by drowning, and he even made it to dry land (in some sense, sanity). Even this doesn't stop the threat of death. Paul and his fellow survivors are collecting wood for a fire, trying to warm themselves. Death changes form and attacks again, this time in the form of a snake. In reading God's Word, I am familiar with this form (Gen. 3:4). However, because Paul obeyed God's Word, death had no place in his life in any form. We must live in obedience to God's Word and never die.

So, you see, my loyalty is not to my cancer-laden flesh but to my heavenly Father who will receive me when my earthly body gives out. Walking into this forest we call life, I am well past the halfway point. Now I am headed out of the forest. I don't expect people who are not in this phase of life to fully understand.

So what happens when you go home and leave all the hospital professionals? No more machines or people monitoring your numbers, just you and what's left of your life. After this, your mind (complete with outside influences) takes over. But this time your mind is much more focused than it's ever been before. This is both good and bad. Bad because now every twinge in your body is amplified, and your mind relates it to cancer pain. Then it seems like these pains never go away, when in all actuality, all you are doing is noticing pains you've had all along but paid no mind to. From now on, suffering is center stage. This is well covered in God's Word (2 Cor. 4:4), blindness of the mind. Just because I invested a majority of my time in my life bringing on this fate doesn't mean a loving and merciful God is not still at work.

This brings me to the good side of my situation. A God that never changes still loves me, and His plans for me have not changed (Jer. 29:11). So, you see, my end will be one ordered by God in perfect love. Even in all sorts of pain and suffering, God still has a plan for every phase of our lives. In my position, most importantly, an expected end. Just writing this makes my joy far overshadow any pain! Christ told me exactly what my end will be (John 14:3). No matter how much we turn our lives into a shipwreck, God's love still applies if we can gather ourselves enough to call on the Lord in total belief and remain faithful to His Word. Sin is separation from God, but His love is unconditional. Hell and the lake of fire were not prepared for humans (Matt. 25:41). I'm not going to force my way into a place where I'm not wanted.

Well, I'm here another day, and God is still good. One by one, I seem to be running into old friends. Some of them look pretty good, but some look worse than I do. They don't have cancer though. So they don't understand me anymore. The continuous cycle of doctors and hospital visits can be a little trying at times, but things could be worse.

I know what happens at four in the morning these days. My body sleeps only when it wants to. At this point, I have no control of life. I'm truly riding the wave of life. I have no idea which way my life is going, but my trust is in God nonetheless. Being a follower of Christ, Jesus said, "If any man follow me he must first deny himself, take up his cross and follow me" (Matt. 16:24). I found out just how valuable self is when my natural strength was gone. I'm grateful that God granted me a space of time with some understanding—understanding I didn't have when self was alive.

Now that I'm dead to self, I see life so much clearer. So denying self is my pleasure. I've always been a powerful man naturally, but within three weeks of being in the hospital, I was as weak as a baby. Strength is seasonal. Self is definitely not my priority. I'm finally realizing that life itself is part of God's glory. I realize my shortcomings (Rom. 3:23).

Dropping sin is so much easier if your goal in life is to glorify God. God is glorified when I am exactly what He created me to be. First a man, then a husband and a father, and all this as a faithful servant. Total surrender to God's will. Instead of a worn-out, dying body, you become a born-again, lively soul.

While some cancer patients live in terror, I live under mercies that are new every morning. Even though there is pain in waking up, the sun shines so much brighter than before. It's like when you lose your sight. Your sense of touch is amplified. I lost the zeal for natural life once I got a view of the amazing spiritual side of life. Now my joy comes from the presence of God in any form. Natural life is enjoyed only when the conditions are favorable. When the conditions change, your joy either decreases or vanishes.

I really do see why King David was a devout, focused man after God's own heart (1 Sam. 13:14). He gave a clue in his writings. He walked through the valley of the shadow of death without fear of evil (Ps. 23). The thing that really gives life to fear in a person's life is sin. When you completely turn your heart away from sin, fear is also a shadow, much like death. I didn't say you won't ever make a mistake, but your heart will never again allow you to sin willingly.

It's actually an outstanding feeling to be able to close your eyes at night and not have to worry about the destruction you reaped the day before. It's called God's peace (John 14:27). This peace belongs to those who obey God. It is one of the many benefits of getting back to God's original creation, His image. Being forced to notice the process of life, how we live day by day and how we were created to live, it amazes me that we call ourselves Christians sometimes.

When life comes to a close, proclaiming yourself a Christian without a life that speaks the same language is useless. When life as we know it comes to an end, the only thing left will be truth. We face truth in the beginning of life, and we will surely face truth again in the end. The middle of life is given to free will.

Coming short of God's glory is probably giving myself too much credit. I wonder if I was even in the ballpark, let alone in the game. I'm fully convinced that God loves me, so my sickness (though painful) is not unto death but unto life eternal. God can heal me completely, but if this means I will get in the way of His glory in my life, I'm good to go. So, you see, denial is very useful in life.

When God looks upon me, He will see the glory that he invested in me (Matt. 25). God's original investment in all of us is life. Some have five talents, some two, some one. I finally found out what that means in life. Real currency is length of life. The servant with five talents had a long life. The servant with two talents had a normal life. The servant with one talent had a shorter life but life nonetheless. God's glory that He gives is good, and we should let the world know that we are blessed by living godly. I wasted a lot of my life in vain pleasure and glory. Imagine my surprise when I asked the Lord what was going on in my life, and the scripture He gave me was "short glory" (Rom. 3:23).

Up to this point, my talent was all but buried in the earth. I was all about living a decent life but not a glorious one, using God-given strength and time only for my purpose. People could tell I went to church, but my master was clearly self—not Satan, self. After I realized this, I began to glorify God for all of my life. The sunny days for joy, the rainy days for growth. Natural prosperity without spiritual prosperity is not so much sin as it is a distraction.

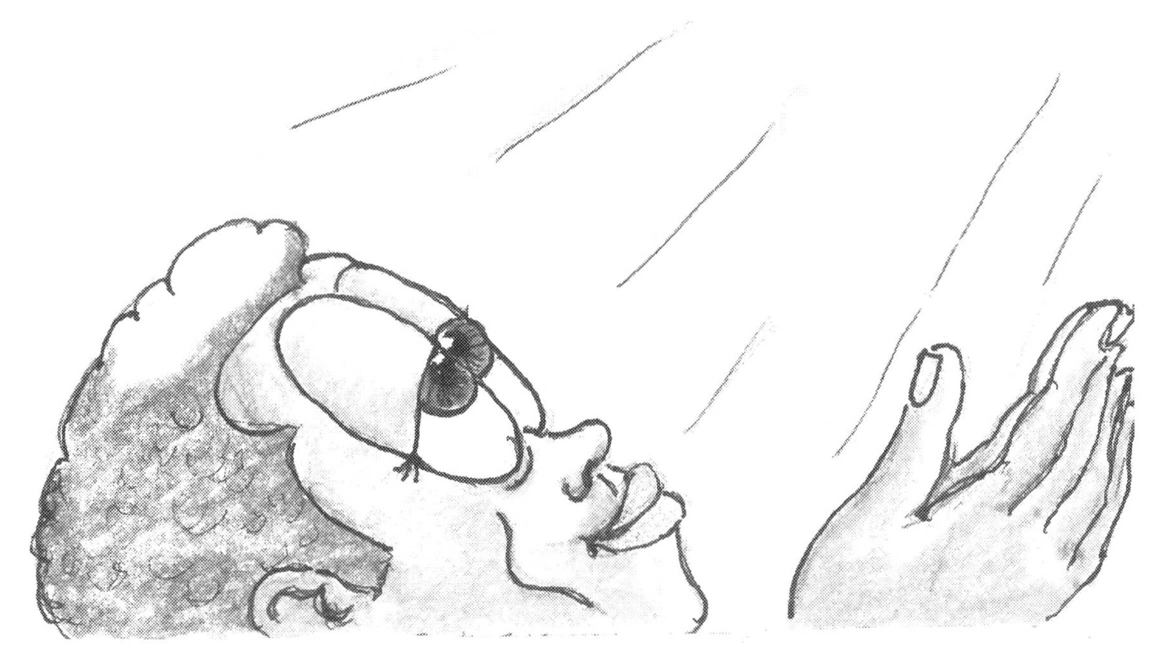

All of this to get my attention. I knew what pleased God from a child. God makes it very plain at the beginning of His Word. It's not difficult; neither is it a big mystery. When God saw the darkness, he simply said, "Let there be light" (Gen. 1:3–4). Light itself was a pleasure to God. Humans love darkness rather than light (John 3:19). In this passage of scripture, I find God's light that was called forth from the beginning (Jesus). The sun was created later; the Son was there in the beginning. The light from heaven that we ignore as long as the sun is shining. The light that my life needs to reflect is the one from heaven (Jesus) (John 1:4).

Just like God approved this light in the beginning, He approved Him also in the New Testament (Matt. 3:17). This light caused the separation of light from darkness, then and now. God's Word does not change. We must live a life of light, seeing that God's Son (Jesus) is His glory, as the Son is the glory or illumination of the Father.

This is the importance of honoring your parents. You are the light others see your parents in. Funny how all this stuff is so unimportant when you're healthy enough to do your own will. I'm so happy that God spared me in time to complete His glory in my life. I'm sick, but nothing keeps me from doing what I used to do except the knowledge that God is not pleased, and I don't have time to waste.

Reality has separated me from a life of foolishness. I don't sit around and wait for death. I started living full speed ahead. I've learned to love in the light and live in the light. Whoever and whatever God sheds light on should be loved. This includes all of God's creation. Hard to do when you feel that everyone else's situations are worse than yours.

Why did God let this happen to me? Why indeed. Ever heard of "Take up your cross and follow Me"? We all have one. It's a matter of whether we choose to bear it righteously or not. We bear one knowingly or not. This all depends on which cross you choose. There were three on the hill that day (Easter). One was for the sins of the whole world, one was self-justification, and the other was for souls like me who are near the end but have gained a place in paradise through the love of Christ.

Just like that repented thief, I must glorify God with what's left of my life. So, life is rough sometimes, but I choose to bear it in Jesus's name. When things got tough near the end, Jesus's flesh said, "Father, if it be your will, take this cup from me." But like Jesus, God is giving me the strength to say, "Nevertheless, thy will be done."

So I have my cross (the very cross that I built with my own disobedience to God) and am bearing it up a hill. The trick to this whole cross thing is God gives you a choice to deal with your sins or not. You can carry a cross to glory or carry one to damnation. "God let" should be taken in the right context. God lets us have our way. Choose your way or a wonderful gift (Rom. 6:23). So you can kind of understand why I choose to accept and cherish this wonderful gift from God.

It took a cross to get that thief close to God. I bear a cross to get me there also. God's own Son was glorified on a cross, but we sometime think just because things get a little rough, God has forsaken us. That same horrible cross made all people look up. Are people looking up because of you?

Now comes the follow Jesus part. Deny yourself, take up your cross. Sounds like a sacrifice that must die. But since Jesus already died for me, I'll become a living sacrifice (Rom. 12:1–2). My life ended in that hospital room. Now I'm more alive than I've been in fifty-six years of life. Following Jesus is a permanent life change and a process. It's like leaving family behind (spiritually) or changing occupations (from fisherman to fisher of men).

Jesus walked so close to his Father that He walked from this present earth to glory. Not that that's an act I can follow. Following is not just about eating the fish and the loaves. There was also the danger, hate, and unbelief. There are those who think my life is in this condition because God is punishing me in some way. This is not so. If you eat something that you know upsets your tummy, and you get an upset tummy, who's punishing whom?

When you are in a place of uncertainty in life, it helps to be on the proven path. There is only one path that is approved by God for humankind, Jesus. We can say whatever we please, but Christ is the only one who walked from earth to glory in complete victory.

Another pain management day. These are a big part of my life these days. They say a wounded dog will strike, but with the knowledge of what is really happening to you, your wounds tend to make you very humble. With all this pain, the sun is shining in my heart, so I must leave my safe comfort zone. I will venture out today to a flea market full of people of all sorts to look at new and old (my favorite) merchandise and to enjoy the kids' smiles.

I have two of my own spoiled grandkids with me. Now to see if I can share some of this "Son" shine God put in me. One of pain's major functions is to cloud up your personality. Clouds block the appearance of the sun, but the light of day still remains. Presenting that daylight is my overcoming victory.

This was God's commandment from the very beginning: "Let there be light" (Gen 1:3). This is the reason for managing pain around others, so they see only the light of day. This is translated as hope. I am not defeated in any way but a son of the almighty God of heaven. I know this sounds crazy, but I'd like to have a funeral where no one has reason to cry.

Another Sunday morning, and I would love to go to church. This involves getting up, showering (which is extra fun, getting around the whole catheter thing), then putting clothes on. I can't wear fancy church clothes anymore because of my condition. So I'll find the clothes that are most comfortable and put them on. I don't think there is anything more annoying than an unpredictable body. Anyway, I did go to church.

Thinking about the remainder of my life, the Spirit makes things perfectly clear. I read a scripture that said Jesus was manifested to take away the sins of the world. Only one way to do that—blood. Imagine that, born to die, the Son of God. Jesus lived thirty-three years preparing to glorify God in death. Funny how people think that this kind of thing can happen to Jesus (the perfect Son of God) but not to us. Manifested means to be displayed. This to me is interesting. So what am I manifested for?

There was a small group of people who believed in Christ until the end. Is there anyone that believes in me? Is there someone following my life? Of course there is. I've never considered myself a good musician, but still, there are a few people who play music today because I did. I never was a great artist, but there are some people out there who are very good artists because of my art. So, believe me, you do have followers.

How critical are my actions even in a hard place in life. If I am in a bad condition, I'll stay home and cry to God. I will not leave home and ruin your day. God said, "Let there be light" (Gen. 1:3). So, when you see me, no matter my condition, I'll bring light!

There is another type of manifestation that comes to mind. A list of goods that are supposed to be in a package (Rom. 14:17). This is the manifestation of the package that Jesus sent to the world after His glorification. We who received that package should possess the same goods. The only righteousness I can claim is the fact that I love God and His Word. This love has been developing through my life. Even though I got into some messy situations in life, it was my knowledge and love of God that kept me out of so many life-destroying situations. Righteousness has a short rope when it comes to questionable situations. It will let you go only so far. The best warning system a person could have is some knowledge of God to lessen the shortness of glory.

The knowledge of God will also make you understand your enemy, Satan, and how his very name means accuser. I can handle rough times, knowing that God commanded light in the life of humankind and the brightness of His glory. Creating humankind and putting them in the best and brightest place on earth, this proved his love for humankind.

In comes the enemy, Satan, the accuser who draws attention to the only potential dark spot in the whole garden. We know this to be the tree of the knowledge of good and evil. I will not allow Satan to draw my attention to the darkest area of my life as long as God is still present and working in my life. "Let there be light." His light still illuminates His creation in me. Cancer is here but on the back burner until God is through with me.

I would never be able to deal with this decaying body without God's wonderful peace in my spirit. At the beginning of this horrible episode, I contracted a strange infection in my bloodstream. I lay in that hospital bed and screamed like a crazy man for three weeks; the pain was just that bad. In all of that body malfunctioning, my mind was at perfect peace. I finally achieved total surrender to Christ. With total surrender comes perfect peace.

If a soldier is wounded badly in war and there is no doctor present, he must surrender to survive. The prison camp has doctors, shelter, food, and water. Everything he needs, not necessarily what he wants. I would love for God to just take all the hurt away, but since I'm a prisoner of a body with cancer, I'll settle for eternal peace from God.

The very first attack I suffered was in the mind. This is where Satan loves to attack us (Eph. 4:23). First thing he says is, "You're going to die." But then I recall all the family and friends who haven't reached my age (without cancer). So he can't threaten me with that. I'm still here. I don't see any unfairness on God's part. I find myself thankful to God. With the Spirit of God, you don't allow yourself to be pushed around by negativity. The key to dealing with a bad body is to have a sound mind.

The joy in my life at this point is strictly in knowing that, because of Jesus Christ, death is just a shadow (Ps. 23:4). Jesus is with me always, even in the valley. I'm fully trusting in God's preparation (John 14:2). All I have to do is make it to death in a state of holiness that is pleasing to God and to be an overcomer (Rev. 2:11). Jesus Christ proved this by raising people from the dead. The ultimate proof was getting up Himself.

Forgive me if I don't cry about going to heaven. You don't have to believe me, but even in this condition, I can feel heaven on earth. Since I've been in this condition, my body has been rough, but my spirit is untarnished by worldliness. You may say this is unimportant, but an excellent spirit is the thing that gives you favor with both God and humankind (Dan. 6:3).

I will strive for the excellent spirit that comes with loving God. In this, you will love everyone else correctly, and this is pleasing to God. To me, the best medicine for an achy body is the laughter of children. So pure and sweet, it gives you a charge of life like a battery charger. My children and grandchildren are very much in love with me because I walk as close as I can with God. I pray for them constantly and love them always. Not to mention a wife that exceeds the very meaning of wife.

My joy is complete in Christ. I wake up every morning to these people that God placed in my life and in my care (I love them like my own soul). We'll talk about Michelle (that spells pure love) later. Right now, I have an overflow of joy!

Let me talk about my big boy for just a few. This guy is my heart. When things went terribly wrong, who would step in when it really counted? Mykal Joe, my oldest son. After the horrible hospital stay, I was reduced from a man who could lift hundreds of pound of weight to being as weak as a baby, not being able to turn over in bed. I was nursing home–bound at fifty-four. But I have the type of son that wouldn't even entertain that idea. He, along with that wonderful lady of his, took me into their home. This lady, my Teenie, my daughter-in-law, who I love very much.

If folks loved half as much as these two, the churches would be full. These two rented everything I needed to function and recover from this shipwreck. They took their time to cook, clean, and push me to exercise, all while going to their regular jobs. They worked overtime to support me through this sickness.

Then my son purchased me a chair that would become the most comfortable spot on earth for me (literally). I am helped by the chair that lifts me to a standing position and also to a very relaxing lying position for sleep. I love the fact that when the doctors were preparing me for death, my son was preparing me for life. Now is the time for the fathers of this generation to envy me because my boys are simply the best.

I know that nourishment of the body is important, but feeding the mind in this condition is just as important, if not more. It's really important to have the right friend in the desert of life—that place where life is not flourishing. Cancer is the beginning of a desert experience. Where things were once plush and green, now life is dry and abrasive. In this desert, there is not enough of anything to sustain natural life. Running out of supplies but still moving forward.

If I didn't understand that life is in God's hands, living would be overrated. There is a big difference between living and surviving. I'm determined to live until I die. I plan to show signs of life every extra day that I am blessed with. Survival is for those who have no God. I'm blessed to not have a pity-party mode. But when pain brings tears, I stay alone so that that part of life is not public knowledge. I am alone right now, and things are a bit painful, and the only reason you know it is because I told you. See? It works. Time for a pain pill. The only person I just can't hide from is my Shell.

This is all really a blessing at times. I'm learning to dwell in the secret place of the Most High (Ps. 91:1). I'm finding myself in places where God's pure love is the only thing relevant. How do you survive the mind game, depression, death threats? Dwell in God's secret place. This is in His favor by obedience and total surrender. Basically, the heart of God. God ordered light, and He was very pleased with the results of that light. We should reproduce it, instead of darkness.

This brings me to my only baby girl. Yes, of course, the love of my life, aside from my Shell. True beauty from the inside out. She is in my prayers because I see Satan wanting badly to stop her simply because she's got it like that. Beloved of God and very talented. Whenever she's used by God, her spirit is simply heavenly. The volume of attacks on her life and family should let her see her exceedingly great value in kingdom business. I still believe I'd be healthy as a horse if I had no true value in God's kingdom.

If people knew their true value, they would never engage in any type of inglorious living. Once this exceptional baby of mine realizes this, she will never be stopped or halted by any person. The only problem is heavenly love has no earthly match. When God has blessed you with this, you often end up unequally yoked with other people. This can leave you friendless for long periods. But you still must be constant and faithful in relationships with other people because this love brings real results. Unequally yoked in this case is not talking about marriage but worldly love and heavenly love.

We are set out as sheep amongst the wolves (Matt. 10:6). The wolf is a natural predator of sheep. This is why we constantly get attacked by people who are not God's sheep. If you're not dealing with wolves, where did you get off track? Some wolves are pets, well trained. Someone with the love of God must teach the love of God. My mom trained a wolf (me) to be a daddy that loves you guys with all his heart.

Big Mac, name courtesy of one of his favorite uncles, Dave. I'll talk about Dave a little later. Back to my Big Mac. Fantastically talented, handsome father of my super pawpawlicious grandson. Still praying that someone will give him a chance in his field of expertise. I am an amateur artist, but Big Mac takes it to another level. I like the fact that when we ride around town, we can see his work on church signs welcoming people into the house of the Lord.

After my big boy and Tennie put me back together again, Mat and his wife, Vicky, had a second baby boy. Shell and I went to Mat and Vicky's house to help with the new baby (I couldn't do much). But when everyone else was busy, they would lay the baby on my chest. I could feel that tiny little heartbeat. It felt like there was a jumper cable from his heart to mine.

That little fellow is a master at melting pain away. The love of a child is so pure, as they are so close to the heart of God. I love this child so much. Then in all this, I hear the voice of God explain the present experiences, saying, "You would give your life for that baby without a second thought. I love you more than you love that precious little child."

I understand that I'm going through this painful wilderness so that I will be able to handle living in the Promised Land. Israel made it to that land, but they were not able to maintain the standard of holy living that it took to remain in that good land.

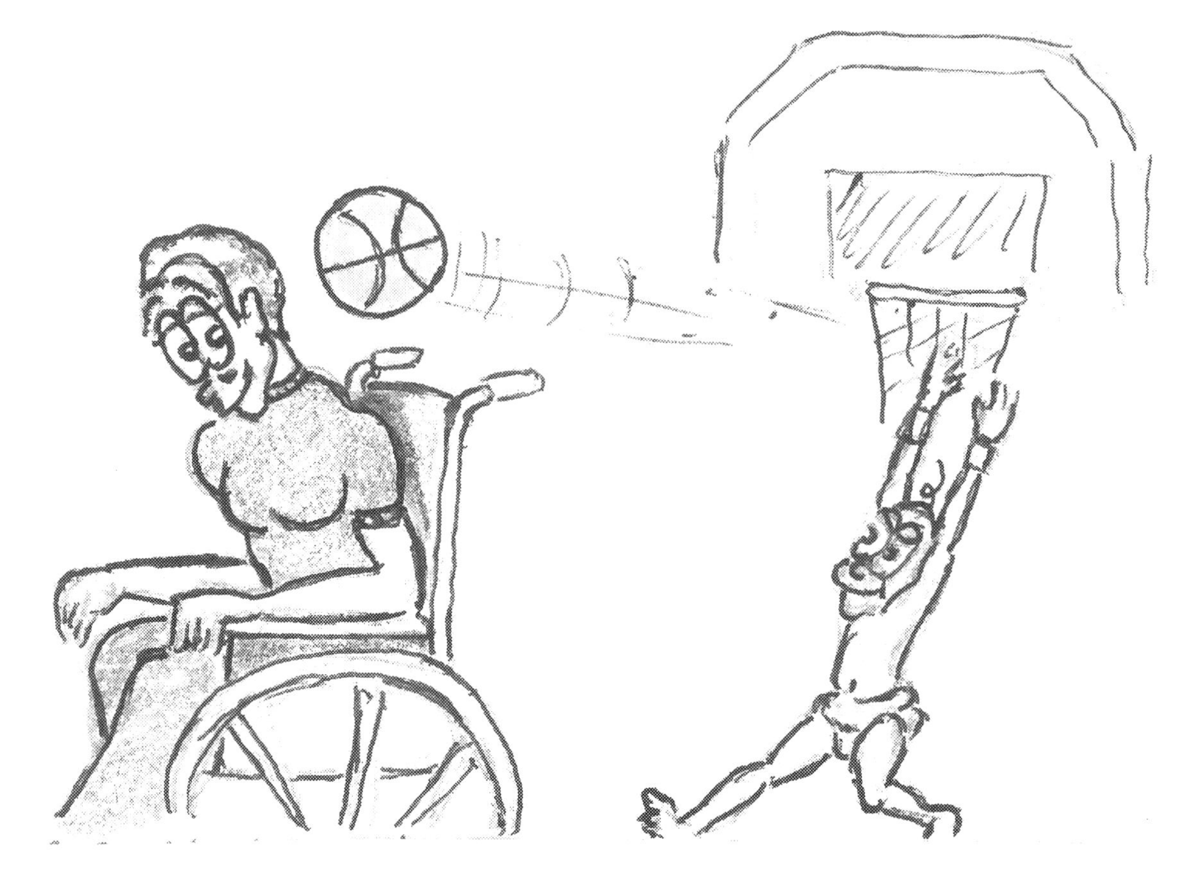

There's also my oldest grandson, my hero, Nik-a-man. My source of power. Nik doesn't know anything about "I can't." When Pawpaw is in pain, Nik says it's time to play basketball. Nik was my daily infusion of faith. There I was trying to catch another breath, then out of nowhere comes a flying basketball to the head. You know, I'm not going to disappoint this handsome little, smiley boy by not playing basketball. I love the little rat. Whenever I don't feel I have the strength to play, Nik has faith that I do (Mark 10:15).

Children never let us forget the innocence in God's spirit and the innocence we once had. Adam and Eve were totally naked. All they saw at first was the glory of God. I think back, trying to remember the last time I looked at a woman and saw what God created instead of body parts that only scream sex.

God creates this masterpiece of beauty just for man, and in no time flat, a jealous, fallen angel tricks us into reducing God's wonderful gift to a sex toy. I like Nik's childish faith. It forces me back to a simple, purer time in life.

This takes me back to God's first purpose for me—to glorify His name (in earth as it is in heaven), to continue His heavenly glory here on earth (Matt. 6:10). I am in God's image as a continuation of his glory here on earth. We have gotten so far away from God's created people that God sends us little boys like Nik to remind us that we were once innocent.

Take a break from dying. Believe it or not, sometimes you don't have time to die. It's two in the morning, and I get a call from my son-in-law. His forty-year-old sister is dead. Being Pawpaw is not just a title but who I am. I have his three girls to deal with, who are old enough to know what death is but not old enough to understand it. So I will stop dying and turn on the voltage love.

This is my girls' aunt on their father's side. Angie, every family has that aunt that keeps you laughing all the time. She just has that great personality that creates smiles. Now this young lady has passed on suddenly and has affected every person in the house. Suddenly my situation seems small and pointless.

I must use every gift that God has made available to me to shed light on this situation (Gal. 5:22). Again, darkness will take a back seat so that I may present the light of God. Problems need real solutions. So I will love as much as humanly possible.

Thought for today: how does death choose his victims? I know God's light is the life of humankind. Do we live as long as our lights illuminate God's creation properly, or is there something else? I loved Angie dearly, but was her light used to brighten the path to the God that lovingly created her?

It's like the five wise and five foolish virgins. We know that we have the oil of life in our lamps (bodies) at the beginning of life. Five of those burned that oil constantly without thought for the future life, almost like they didn't expect the oil to run out at some point. When the wise know that abundant life is available, they make preparations for such times by obtaining extra oil (the Holy Ghost), God's eternal spirit that guarantees life everlasting.

So you can see, if not properly maintained and refueled, a person's light could simply go out. The big deal with this whole journey that we call life is that God has fully provided us with everything that we need to make this portion of our trip (Phil. 4:19). When humans couldn't find bread in the wilderness, God rained down bread from heaven. This was good for that generation, but this generation doesn't usually have a shortage of natural bread, rather a shortage of spiritual nourishment. People these days lack content of character. Mostly the God image.

This creates short glory. We must figure out a way to reflect God's image in a dark world by our lives saying, "Let there be light." Every lamp that goes out is a reminder that you need extra oil. In layman's terms, every death is a lesson in life. Without God's spirit, we often don't have the wisdom to take these lessons. God has no pleasure in seeing humankind suffer. Suffering is the result of sin (Rom. 6:23). Plain and simple, wages must be earned. What exactly are you working for in life?

I get back to dying now (Phil. 1:21). You must read this scripture to fully understand that statement. Cancer is causing me to die out in a spiritual sense much more rapidly than natural death. They say that when God shuts a door, He opens another one. This is a faithful saying. But it's spiritual. Many doors closed in my natural life that will never open again. No need to live in the past. It is counterproductive.

You see, a death sentence in Christ means a transformation from this body to something closer to God's image. This reflects in my thoughts as well as my actions. So there is no fear of dying in me right now. This whole thing is changing me into something closer to God. Realizing this leaves me no room for doubt.

You can see where some knowledge of God stabilizes you in hard times. It's amazing that I function even better these days than I did before I got sick (mentally). I have no confidence in flesh. I'm finding that a strong spirit takes good care of a body that is subject to it. This is the way God planned it, seeing that God is a spirit. Our spirit is the thing that connects us to the God of all heaven and earth. My flesh was never created to control my life.

I'm reminded that life itself is light from God. How in the world can flesh control that? Satan had me thinking I was in control. But spirit depressed by the flesh is totally out of control. In our flesh, we have the biggest case of "I can't help it." This creates rapists, murderers, drunks, drug addicts, and so on.

Change out day. This time, it's a few days after my birthday. This is a medical procedure that takes forty-five seconds on a good day. That hurts like I'm being cut in half. God is blessing me even in this department. I used to fight depression the whole week of change out. There is something about knowing that extreme pain is unavoidable that troubles the human mind. Take this cup from me, right (Mark 14:36)?

You may wonder why I use scripture so much. Because everything we do has a natural side and a spiritual side. Scripture explains the spiritual side of my situation. Spiritual is life; natural is death. We can see death plainly, but we don't always see life. It took a long time for me to see life in all this pain.

In this, God sent me one doctor (Dr. Eric Kuhn) who can do this quickly and correctly. Others have tried, and I ended up in the hospital usually in more pain and infected. Today was painful but blessed. Twenty seconds, done and out the door. Thank God this only happens once every six weeks. Pain meds make me sleep for hours, then low, throbbing pain wakes me for another round.

In all of this, my peace remains intact, perfect in the Lord Jesus Christ. This is also me exercising my free will, as I choose to live in the freedom of perfect love and not the shadow of pain. My pain is a shadow because Christ has already overcome it, and I am in Christ.

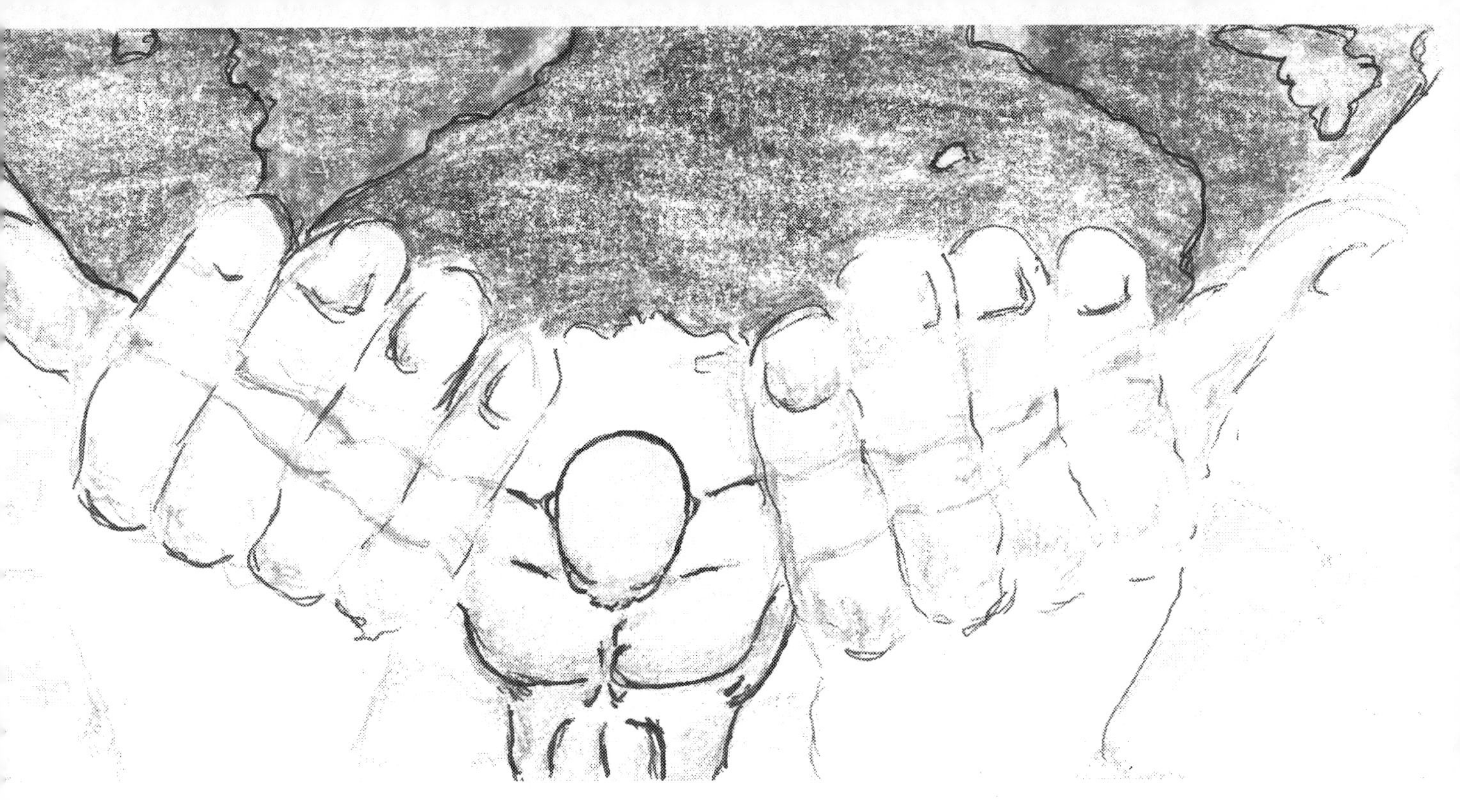

You would think cancer is enough, but if you have people who are attached to your heart, guess what? Any time something happens to one of them, you have an irregular heartbeat. Shortly after change out, my son (son-in-law) lost his sister in death. He is a strong, young man and the very best of his generation. To watch him suffer this way is very painful.

At this point, father-in-law gives way to just plain father. This man has lost four family members in four months. He is the pillar of his family, so I watch him stand in the time of trouble, leaning on the God that his family does not see. The strongest men in the world are actually leaning on God. Samson's strength was displayed physically, but when things got rough, he had to call on God (the Spirit) for real strength (Judges 16:28).

There are so many things that happen in a day that make me totally forget that I have cancer. This sounds crazy, but it's very true that some of the things that life brings to you are worse than death. Seems most parents would rather be dead than bury their children or watch them suffer. With help from God, I know that after this storm, my son will return to us stronger than he's ever been, with more character.

Life is only one big force. It's all around us. We are responsible for how we flow through it and how it flows through us. Satan's main objective in the world of humankind is to pollute or stop that flow.

I am reminded of a situation where Jesus (the perfect flow between God and humanity) told Peter after Peter walked with him awhile, "Satan desires to have you and to sift you as wheat" (Luke 22:31). To me, Jesus told Peter, "Now that you are flowing with life (John 15:1), Satan wants to break that flow and get you all stressed out with the many distractions and divisions in natural life."

Is this son of mine out of the storm yet? Not on your life. Just days go by or hours, however you want to look at it. In comes another wave of mass destruction. I'm not going into detail on this one because there are other people involved, but believe me, it's a real downer.

These are moments when I'm glad my hope is built on nothing less than Jesus's blood and righteousness. People get shot over these offenses. In the Bible, a stoning would be proper.

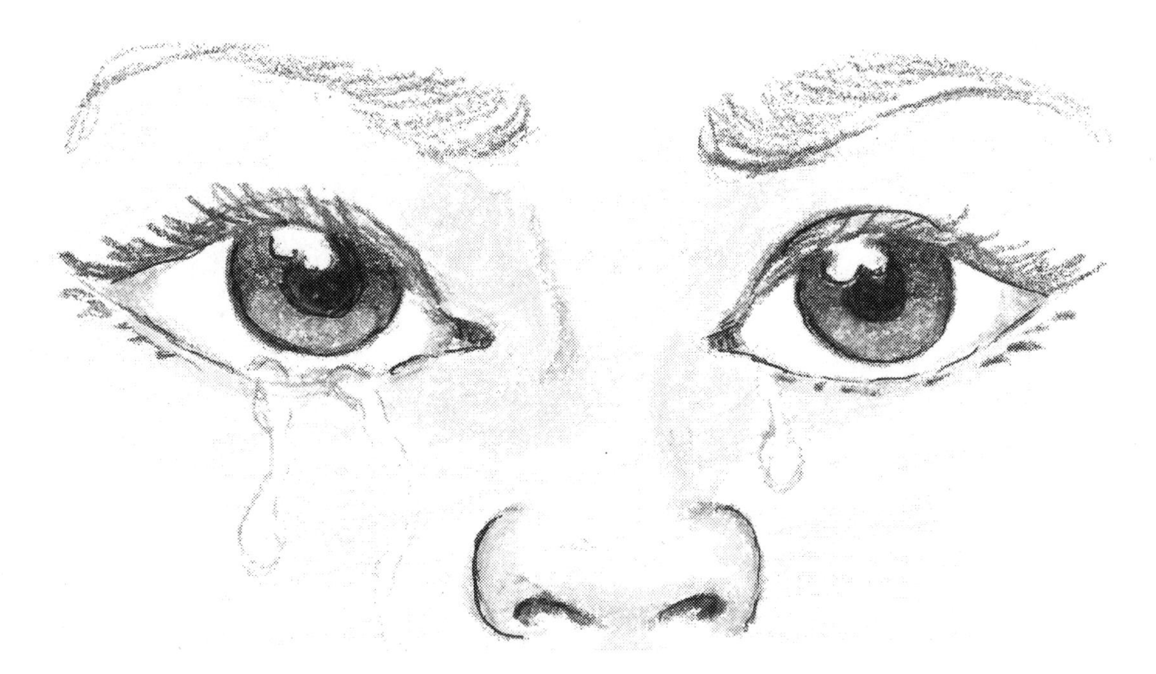

This offense is the most destructive one against girls and women. Life-changing, inerasable, mind-wrecking things that could happen to females. It opens the door to all sorts of nasty spirits in the female mind. We men don't realize that the worst thing we can do is mistreat God's personal gift to us, women. Sad that this is considered normal these days.

If we bother to look, there are so many things that happen in a day's time that completely overshadow our personal issues. I understand why Jesus said, "You must first deny yourself" (Matt. 16:24). If I concentrate on my problems, I will miss out on the rest of my life, in Christ.

I know that in my state, I'm living on borrowed time. You don't borrow time to waste it. I can either sit in the middle of my situation, or I can give whatever I've got left to the world around me. Darkness makes light brighter. When night falls, the only thing you notice is the lights. When man-made lights are put out, there are lights in the heavens.

I'm saying this because of what happened to my beautiful granddaughter. I can't really explain due to subject matter, but it was a potential disaster. God is still having mercy on my family in spite of our shortcomings. Good looks and a great body are a curse without a heavenly mind.

All of this is happening in a three-day period, from Friday to Sunday night. However, on Monday morning, I receive my new mercies from the God that I love. With the morning comes the most excellent glory of God breaking through with the sunshine. I'm the one with the sickness, but my Shell seems to suffer more than I do. Today, God has put a big, beautiful smile on her face. This, to me, is personal sunshine. I love her smile.

After all that we went through, God has allowed us to pay for a cruise and buy round-trip plane tickets. All this on one paycheck. I'm not able to work anymore. We are cruising to Alaska, something she has always wanted to do. I've been married to Shell for thirty-seven years, with plenty of ups and downs. Sometimes you don't know why you're working so hard to build your marriage. This is why. So that you'll have personal sunshine after life's terrible storms. Jesus is the lily of the valley, but He also gives us personal lilies that remain beautiful in any dark valleys. That's my Shell. Not being able to work, I gave up a lot of stuff. I don't sit around and think about what I don't have because what I do have is a wonderful God that manifests Himself in everything I do have, including my Shell.

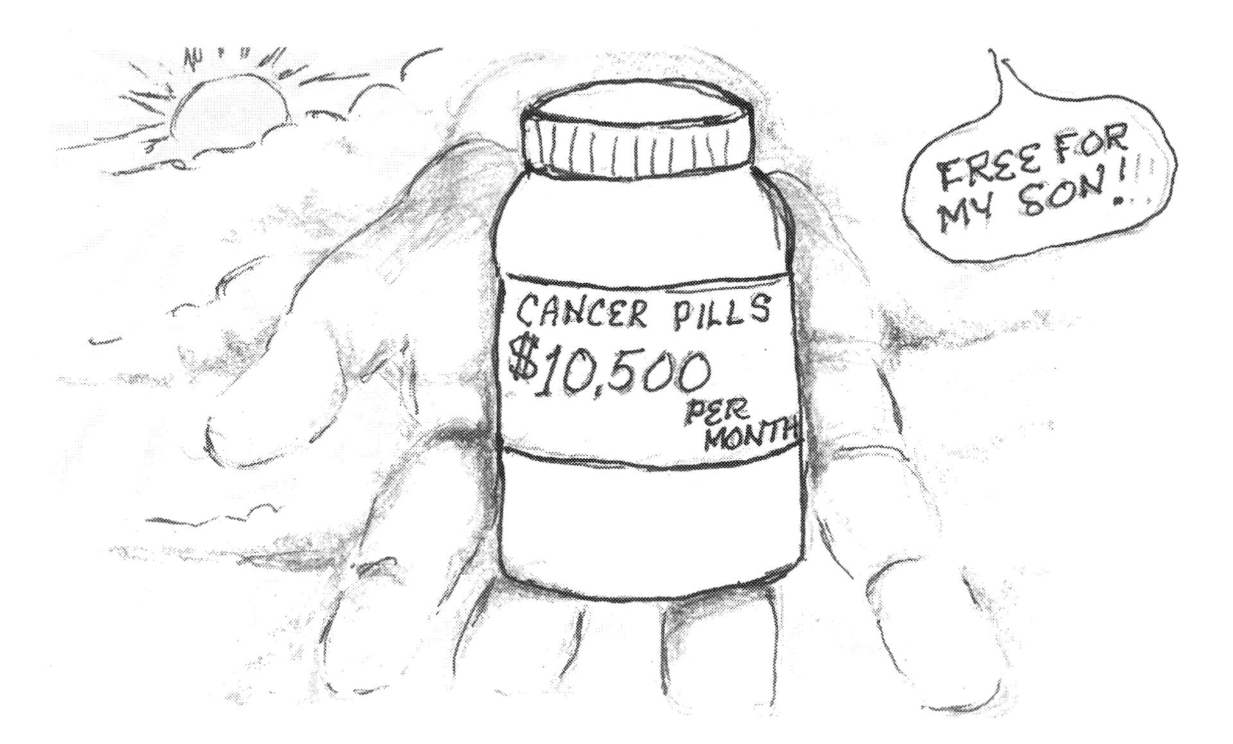

God is so incredibly good. No matter what I need, it always comes from somewhere. I had been out of my cancer meds for four months because a one-month supply cost $10,500. This is just one bottle of pills. I've been blessed with a great doctor (Dr. Andrew Parchman) who understands my struggle. He told me, "I can't afford that," and he's a doctor! Imagine me trying to buy these pills, and I have no job. But God. My favorite phrase. His Word trumps all others. He allowed my doctor to find a way to get me these pills for free for one year.

Look at that. I can actually afford to live for one more year. For those who hate me, sorry, not yet. God has spoken a Word over my life. I will live and not die. If this body gives up today, boy have I lived since God sent His Work through a woman of God. She came to me at my son's house just to bring a Word from God. Since then, my spirit has been soaring to heavenly levels.

If you don't do anything else in life, get a Word from God. Everything around you may be dying, but you can live by God's Word. Miracles are simply God's spoken Word. That is what a miracle is, my friend. Say hello to one of God's miracles, me. Years after my death sentence, I have things and go places that I couldn't afford when I worked two jobs. All this is on top of abundant life.

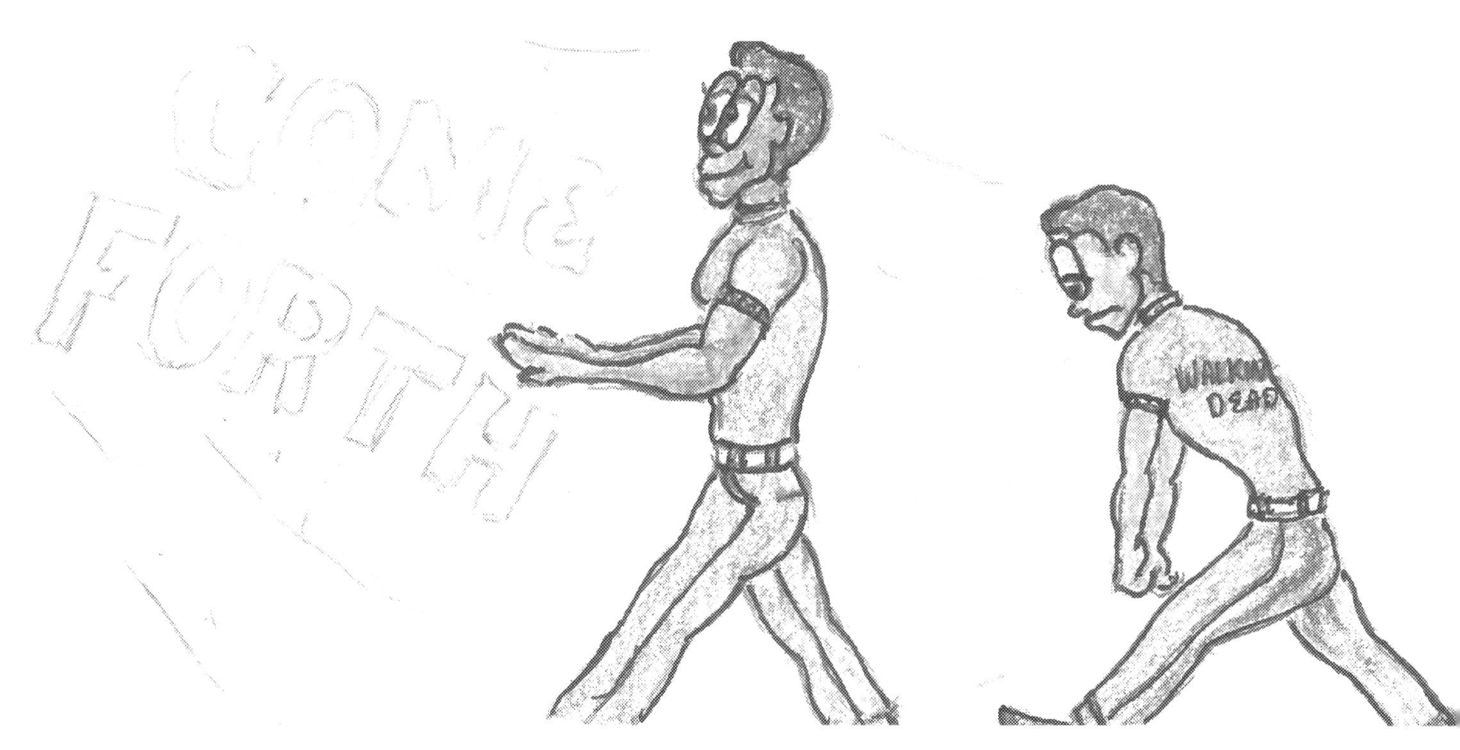

The truth is that I was in a state of death before cancer opened my eyes. Many people are in a deep sleep or state of death. This allows them to get comfortable in sins and trespasses against God. Comfort in this state leads to eternal damnation. You see, through sickness, God would not suffer my soul to be lost to a state of blind living, which is a state of death.

This is a battle that no devil or demon could ever win, for it is the will of God (2 Pet. 3:9). This is called the Lazarus effect. People said that Lazarus was dead, and in my life, pretty much things were dead. Church was hitting on nothing. Family was all grown up, living their own lives. Marriage had its up and downs, and on the downs, Satan and every other enemy in the universe attacks heavily.

So many of these attacks are successful because of our lack of knowledge about what love and marriage really are. The worst mistake in the world is selling something that you don't understand for a low price. Then finding out that it was priceless (marriage) in God's sight. You may live through a divorce, but know that you've cut your godly favor in half. This makes me grateful that God called my spirit back to me like He did with Lazarus, and my marriage was kept alive.

Every day, that first huddle of pain in the bathroom is the main one of the day. After that, I can function with the normal stuff. There are certain things that people do daily that are a real struggle for me now. My strength is still very low after all this time. I guess I shouldn't expect too much.

Most mornings, it's just me and my Shell in the house. We get up, say, "I love you, kiddo," and then start preparing for our day. After cleaning up a bit, she prays before starting work. I sit up in my chair and pray with her. After this, she gets things going at her desk and fixes us both a cup of coffee. Then she pulls back the curtain and floods the room with God's glorious light.

When the light comes in, darkness must flee. I'm blessed with another day, proving that any victory death has is subject to God's Word. This is the same God that loves me, so this is a day that the Lord has made. Currently rejoicing and being glad. Kind of corny sounding, but I get through disaster by focusing on the Master.

The best way to learn to appreciate a day is to have the doctor say, "You don't have any days to spare." I've been told I'm dying; meanwhile, I watch people I know die without warning. So sad to die unprepared. So, instead of being foolish, I'll spend the rest of my time glorifying my heavenly Father as I'm on my way home.

Every day of our lives, we should be learning more about our Creator and ourselves and how they go together. We must learn how to reconnect to our life source, which is God's Spirit. Humans become living souls only when God supplies the life. A new opportunity comes with every daybreak. Satan would have us focus on flesh that is tied to dust rather than our connection with God.

We connect by listening to different preachers every day. Not everyone is preaching the truth, but you can't learn to fight an enemy if you don't know who he is. You may say, "I know who my enemies are." Wrong. Number one, there is an "s" on the end of enemies. Number two, if you are constantly hating or fighting people, you have not yet begun to fight your real enemy.

Not being afraid of life really helps when you're trying to live. Knowing your enemy and his abilities is a vital part of life unless the Spirit says no. I will listen to anyone to see where they are. They are either for God or against God. There is no middle ground. Some feel that self is the middle ground, but it is not so. You cannot please God in self (John 3:6, 4:3).

This life forces you to love yourself, put yourself first. Sounds like a great idea. Too bad it leads to self-gratification at any cost. The price is usually family, friends, your marriage, and finally your soul.

I rise in the morning like a Frankenstein monster. I think the pain is what shocks me back into life. I endure the pain because afterward life itself is a brilliant spectrum of light. It's awesome seeing and hearing life the way God created it and not just by my polluted senses. My senses gave all sorts of limits, tainted by my surroundings and situations.

My perception has always been personal (selfish) and off, but when you get to a place where self is not your center, your perception changes. Now you can actually see what's around you. Self is basically a bulldozer. You plow through life leveling everything in your way (brings things to your level), not really caring who or what you destroy.

Your perception changes, and you begin to weigh everything in the balance of life instead of just pushing weights around. Your goal now is to bring balance to every situation you meet. People are tormented with fear because something has put them out of balance. You may say cancer is a heavy sickness (weight), but it takes different amounts of weight to balance out different people.

Don't let yourself get out of balance. Then maybe your weight won't be quite as heavy as mine. Trouble comes when God takes His hand off of yours (2 Chron. 32:31). When you get too far, God will try your free will to see what's in your heart. This is why you need a pure love for God without wavering—because it will be tried.

Skip the morning pain, today I'm all alone. My girls have a women's day at church. Glad that they have some time away from the obvious story unfolding at home. Even though in Christ, it always looks worse than it is. God's plan is ugly only to the human eye. God obviously prefers beauty over ugliness, light over darkness, and good over bad every day. Why in the world would anyone accuse Him of wrongdoing of any kind?

I think I mentioned it before, that when God was done creating, humankind was in a perfect state of paradise. This was His first thought of humankind (me and you), and these are His thoughts now (Jer. 29:11). I don't like picking one scripture out of a whole passage because it's hard to get the full meaning of that one scripture.

This passage of scripture was letting Israel know that they were going to suffer the consequences this time for their sins. So settle down and live through it. This is more than fair, seeing that the wage of sin is death. God, in His mercy and grace, let them know that you will go through, but you still have a future in God. I love Him so. I still have a future!

I get things done when I'm alone. Today, after mentally sweeping out of my mind all the cancer threats, it's time to clean up my room. I don't believe in letting Shell do everything. She works, so I do whatever I can. This means cleaning everything that I can in a wheelchair of course. I don't have the strength anymore like I used to, so I try to compensate. There is only so much you can do in a wheelchair.

No one here to see how handicapped I really am. No matter how much noise the TV makes, my mind shouts louder. These days, it's very sober and very clear. Sober means not drunken by anything in this life that distracts you from seeing real life (spiritually). By saying this, I mean that my main goal in what's left of this life is to please God at any cost. Pleasing God brings pleasure to my whole family.

Good day or bad day, it all depends on where your joy actually comes from. The joy of the Lord is my strength. Studying the whole passage of scripture, you will find that it's not just jumping and shouting but also understanding the Word of God (Neh. 8:10).

I take joy in still being a positive force in this condition. It is a huge blessing. I want to be functional until the very end. I'm believing God for this blessing.

Mother's Day weekend, and even though my mother has gone home, I still have very fond memories of her. No shortage in beauty and holiness there. Love was plentiful, and the sweetest human spirit ever seen. It's a good thing Shell spent a lot of time with Mom because at times she acts just like Mom. Her sweetness tips the chart, along with her caring heart.

How do I show appreciation to such a wonderful person? I know. After her favorite candy, I'll cook her favorite meal. When I was well, I used to love cooking for her. So today, I'm frying chicken wings in a wheelchair for my love. A labor of love.

This Shell of mine has exceeded expectations in every category of womanhood. A mother whose children simply adore her. Her sons and daughter love her the same and are spoiled by her sweet spirit. I don't know about other men, but I love a godly woman with that sweet, quiet spirit that's always looking for an empty room to fill up with her love. Mother, she is.

There is also that missing mother-in-law spot that she fills, and that is a hard job. Shell pulls it off nicely spiritually. I also play in her hair just like I used to play in Mom's beautiful silver hair. I lay my head on her breast when I'm in pain, kiss her on her warm cheeks for comfort, and hug her tightly for that motherly warmth that I miss from Mom.

The day after Mother's Day, Shell and I are blessed with the presence of not one but two little angels for a sleepover. They are a handful but Mawmaw and Pawpaw's own little slices of paradise. The first to draw attention to the day light was my Veo. Moring pain doesn't have a prayer when Veo is around. From the time he wakes up to the time I wipe his handsome little face, I am hooked.

Veo is not a morning baby. He's moody and hungry. I always keep a snack for my babies. After Veo snacks, he flashes that award-winning smile, and it's off to the races. He finds something that works for drumsticks and beats a tune on the nearest thing. That could be the table, two books, a glass jar, or the window.

That's my Veo, the most fabulous boy ever. I don't know if it's right to love someone this much. I don't know how to explain it, but this little guy who wears me out is my lifeline. I feel so alive when he's here. If I had the strength, I'd keep him with me all the time. Well, here comes Mom to take my Veo home. Guess I should let him go. Love you, boy!

That brings me to the one and only Nik-a-man, my basketball-handling, ankle-breaking grandson. First boy. What can I say? I love this guy. He has the greatest imagination I've ever heard of. Nik is so fun and funny, no to leave out handsome. His smile is day changing. If I'm having a tough day, Nik can cure that, and all it costs me is a snack.

I think it may be snacks that fuel that smile of his. Shortly after that snack, it's time for a game of hoops. There is a basketball hoop on my bedroom door. I didn't know this was going to sentence me to a life of Nik-a-man games. Life could be worse.

He's growing up far too fast. Every time I see him now, he looks more and more like his other nickname, Little Man. I love that boy. He's a pint-sized walking bottle of happiness. Now that he's the ripe old age of six, he hangs out with his friends, so Mawmaw and I don't get to see him so much. I do a lot of staying in the same place these days, and that's just not enough excitement for Nik. These grandbabies are so easy to love. They love to put their faces close to mine. Smiles that close are beautiful. I love the gleaming life in their pretty little eyes. This happens every day when they enter my bedroom.

My wife and baby girl will be taking a trip to Maine together without me. First time ever we have been apart for four straight days. It may sound crazy, but I thank God for the blessing; in a day when mothers and daughters hate each other, my favorite women still love each other with a godly love. People think that they are sisters. They look alike, walk alike, and talk alike, and they are always together. Not so popular these days. It looks good though.

Of course, the trip put me in a lonely spot. In this case, I depend largely on my Bible and getting closer to my Savior. Quiet time to pray, listen, and think about what it is that I'm dealing with and what I'm doing. There are certain parts of my situation that are above my pay grade, so I don't even try to figure it out. Life and death are God's territory, and that's a battle I'll let him fight (2 Chron. 20:15). This is a really good scripture. This king was facing an army that he could in no way defeat. So he turned to the one he served faithfully for help (Jesus, like I did). The serving part is very important, as you need a relationship with Him to enjoy His benefits.

I didn't wait until I was sick to have a relationship with God. I've had a love for Him since I was a child. Boy, am I ever glad. I have not been perfect, and being disobedient kept me from reaching for perfection all my life. Now I'm in finishing school.

This is God's latest cure for what ails me. She's so completely precious that pain cannot overcome her beauty. Pawpaw's last angel. If you ever get cancer, find people to love. No law in nature overrides pure love. The more of God you find in your present situation, the better your days go. Nothing closer to the heart of God (I think) than an innocent child.

If you have children, don't just give them love; pour it on them until they beg you to stop. Not only do you live through your children, but there are healing powers in the love and success in life. You sleep really well when you know your babies are doing well on all fronts. I love you, little girl.

My little Veo. The walking sunshine in Pawpaw's life. He sings his own personal song that brings a smile to my face every time I think of it. They say he's bad. I say he's a little sample of God's pure love. He is the ultimate gift from Mat and Vicky, along with my Nik and Brini girl. All this when I need a little something to live for. Not time to go to heaven, so God gave me a little heaven on earth.

If it is God's will, I would love to stick around for a while and see what becomes of this beautiful boy.

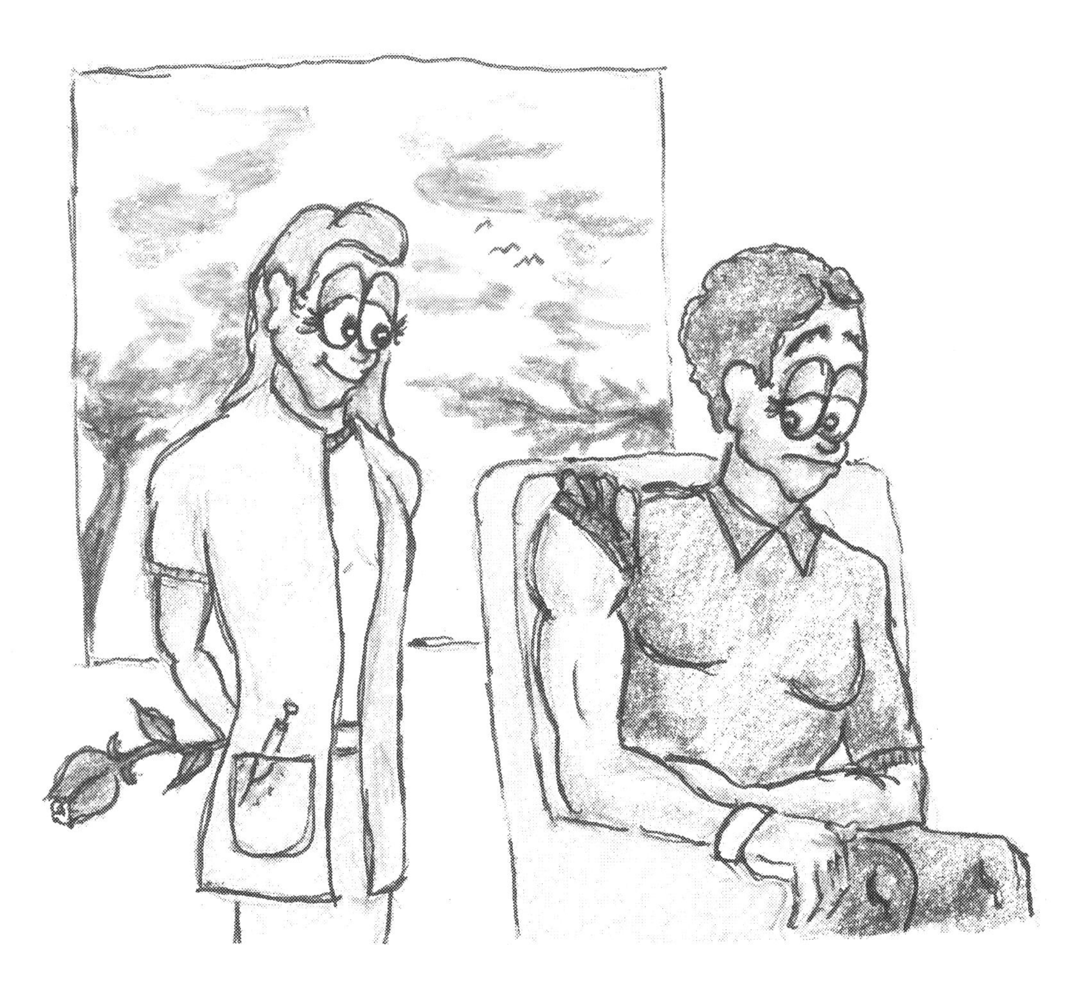

Shot day, how fun. This morning, I forgot to numb up. It's a one-inch needle with a hook on the end. I guess a major ouch is in order here. Kymmie is about to faint because of the amount of blood. Me? I'm used to it. At least I'm not alone today. It's a blessing to have someone with you at a doctor's appointment. Loneliness always makes it worse.

I don't dread going to the doctor because my doctor and his staff are great, upbeat, and very positive—not to mention excellent at what they do. They don't treat you like a death row inmate. It's great to know that others know the process of life and treat you according to this knowledge along with their professional knowledge. I love these people like family. They treat me like family.

Cancer is not necessarily the end of life, but it certainly highlights your mortality. Please understand that this is not the time for depression, not at all. It's like a beautiful flower also created by a wonderful God. The flower makes its way from a seed buried in the ground. It grows for a time. It's not much to look at, and some even grow thorns along the way. In its stages, it goes through storms of wind and rain. This only serves to strengthen its root in the earth (gives it character) and establishes its place in the world (just like us).

The thing is we really don't see what God intends for that flower to be until it reaches its full glory (we call it the end), when the flower blossoms into a beautiful rose. This happens right before it withers up and dies. I'm in my stage of glory right now. I don't know how long my flower will continue to bloom, but I intend to display its beauty until there is no more. Hopefully someone will dry me out and put me in their photo album.

Now that I have cancer, all eyes are on me in the family, giving me a captive audience. It's up to me what I present to them. Have you ever seen a lightbulb blow out? I have. It gets very bright, brighter than it ever was in its normal life. Then suddenly one last burst of light, and it's out.

I believe in God's holy Word, and His first Word concerning me was "Let there be light." This light was to illuminate what God created, not what humankind became (Gen. 1:3). I love God's version of me, not cancer's run-down, sick, tired, and grumpy version. So I will let there be light.

I will not shine any light on or glorify cancer in any way. As long as God allows me to have life, I will glorify life and life only. Death is the end of time; therefore, I have no time for death.

I know my body is coming to its end, but I'm so much more than just a body. I'm a husband to a wonderful woman that I love more each day simply because of who she is. Funny thing about that. Before my body started downhill, I could focus only on the female gift from God in natural ways. Now that things aren't so perfect naturally, my spiritual understanding and sight are very clear. I don't see her as the woman the world says she is but the woman God made her to be. She's beautiful.

I'm a father to three intelligent, spoiled children, and I think there are none better on earth. I'm an elder but not religious. I'm Holy Ghost filled, which is a book in itself.

So, you see, though my body is slipping away, it's freeing up many other parts of life. It's making available to me wonderful insights and discoveries that you just can't see with self in the way. Selflessness is a wonderful virtue that many never get the chance to enjoy. Praise God! Loneliness and depression would eat me alive, but I don't have time for either. I'm on God's good graces, and they don't fit. I've never been rich in money, but God has made me very rich in love. Since he is supplying this love, I will continue to spend it.

Sickness happens not only to the person with the disease but also to the people that love you. It's one of Satan's mind tricks, to spread darkness and depression among your loved ones. No one can pity me unless I'm pitiful. I refuse to be a draw on life. I prefer to be a source of life. Some say that they don't believe in God and eternal life, yet there are loved ones in our lives that live on in our hearts and minds until the day we leave this world.

We actually spend all our lives preparing for this moment. Show business calls it the big finish. This doesn't mean I die today. It means I have time to prepare those I know and love to deal with my physical absence and embrace my spiritual presence. Because of the influence they had in our lives, we feel the presence of Mawmaw and Pawpaw even now.

True love never dies. This is why I prefer to love over anything else. People tend to remember those moments in life where someone showed love when they didn't deserve it. This is why I love Jesus Christ so much. His great love is my connection to our wonderful God.

There are three who watch everything I do. They are very close to my heart. My first grandbaby, Kymberlei, my second, Koreynne, and my little princess, Kamylle. These are Pawpaw's baby girls. I don't know how to process the thought of leaving them, but at the same time, I hope that they will love God and remember all that Pawpaw has shown and told them.

I hope that somehow God will lead them to men who can see how wonderful they really are and not just see body parts. They are beautiful, but beauty can be a blessing or a curse. It's not good for a young lady to have a heavenly body without a heavenly mind. They are cute baby girls to me, but to men of the world, they are targets. They need to know guys, and I'm one of the only guys they trust. We must talk openly. I don't want my leaving to ruin any part of their lives. I need them to carry the love, wisdom, peace, and joy that was Pawpaw's every day of their lives. This is my gift to my precious angels. They were placed in my life just for these times. Now I have even more faith in God.

Look at me. Out of the house today by myself. This is a strange feeling, seeing as Shell takes me everywhere. My body is rebelling against the heat, and there is no comfortable seating in this place. So, with these bones of mine, it's a sacrifice. But Shell's car needs new tires, and they close before she gets off from work.

Don't get me wrong. I'm not complaining, but to be real and transparent, I do have symptoms of my sickness. God's not always going to remove these, but He gives you power to go through in a godly, glorious fashion. That's good enough for me. It's not about me being happy all the time; it's about me being consistent all the time in spite of pain and bad situations. This shows the image of God that we possess.

Who I am is powerful enough to love people, even when I don't feel good. All praise to God and not any religion. I'm not saying don't go to church; I'm saying bring God with you. Don't even try to piggyback off of someone else's walk with God. He is a personal Savior. If I did that, I'd be somewhere preparing to die when God said live.

At this point in my life, I'm not endorsing any church or religion, although these are good for gaining a basic knowledge of an all-powerful God. It's like school. What good is a lesson that you never put into practice? You can't stay in school forever. Church is not wrong, but you can get into a comfort zone where the spirit will move on, and you're still sitting in the same place. Love is progressive and not traditional.

Every single day, God does this wonderful, magnificent performance on mercy and grace that is not recognized or seen by many churches or religions. How is it that people continue to hate when God allows you to take another breath of polluted air and drink a cold glass of water that has all sorts of bad chemicals in it, yet your body processes it and you keep going? We do all sorts of things that are outside of the glory of the God whose image we bear. Yet we close our eyes in sleep, getting as close to death as a person can get every night. When morning comes with a symphony of golden sunlight, and nature is praising God, here we are once more. I prefer to have nothing to do with sin and will glorify this wonderful God.

At the beginning of this episode, nights were kind of shaky. Closing my eyes for long periods of time wasn't actually fun until I thought about who has the power over life and death. Then I thought, *Oh yeah, passing in my sleep would be peaceful and painless*, victory on my side. So if I close my eyes, peace comes. If I wake in the morning, God's mercy meets me with the rising of the sun, leaving no victory for death at all.

I really love knowing who I am and who I will become (1 John 3:2). Death not only has no power over me, but he doesn't even have a key to his own front door (Rev 1:18). These days, I sleep very well. All through the day, I try to live a life pleasing to God so that I can lie down in peace, rather than sleep that is part-time or permanent. One of the many benefits of loving and not hating.

Even at this time in my life, I refuse to live below my privilege as a son of the Most High God. Not even sickness can erase my royalty (in God of course). I love life, and that's why I choose it eternally.

Today is not one of my best. Pain in the midsection, no real feeling in my feet. Cancer folk know this drill. Anyway, it's Sunday, and I can't make it to church. I wouldn't be able to sit that long, so here I am alone again. However, being me, I have to have a preached Word from God. God speaks to me all week long, but on Sunday, I love a church atmosphere. Quick solution: there are a number of good preachers on TV. I'll listen to one of my favorites. This is good for my mental strength.

I am a huge fan of spiritual reinforcement at this point. What's left of me is spirit. I'm not interested in a religious ritual, only a close relationship to God, seeing as rituals do very little for pain.

Don't get me wrong. I love a church where people love the Lord and will help people like me keep my head straight. Whatever controls your mind controls you. I will not allow pain to be my master, but through God's wonderful spirit, I will master my pain. I love my church family, but my confidence is in Jesus Christ.

I think people worry about death too much. Sure, it's coming; nobody get out alive. Not your body anyway. Abundant life is a spiritual thing and a choice. If you allow your spirit to die, you are dead at that very moment, basically just waiting for a grave to open up. If you notice, sickness is not what causes death; loss of spirit is. The body remains alive as long as you have a spirit.

I'm living in the spirit that is eternal. So whenever God sees fit to release me from this failing body, I will continue on with Him and leave all this pain behind. The negative and hurtful things that we go through in life are designed to break our spirits. There are great examples of this in God's Word. The story of Joseph is one (Gen. 37).

We are free to place our confidence wherever we please (Heb. 10:35). If my confidence was in my health and ability to work for my family, I'd be in big trouble right now. My confidence is in Jesus Christ and righteousness. Jesus Christ is for my soul. The righteousness is so that I love and treat everyone I meet justly.

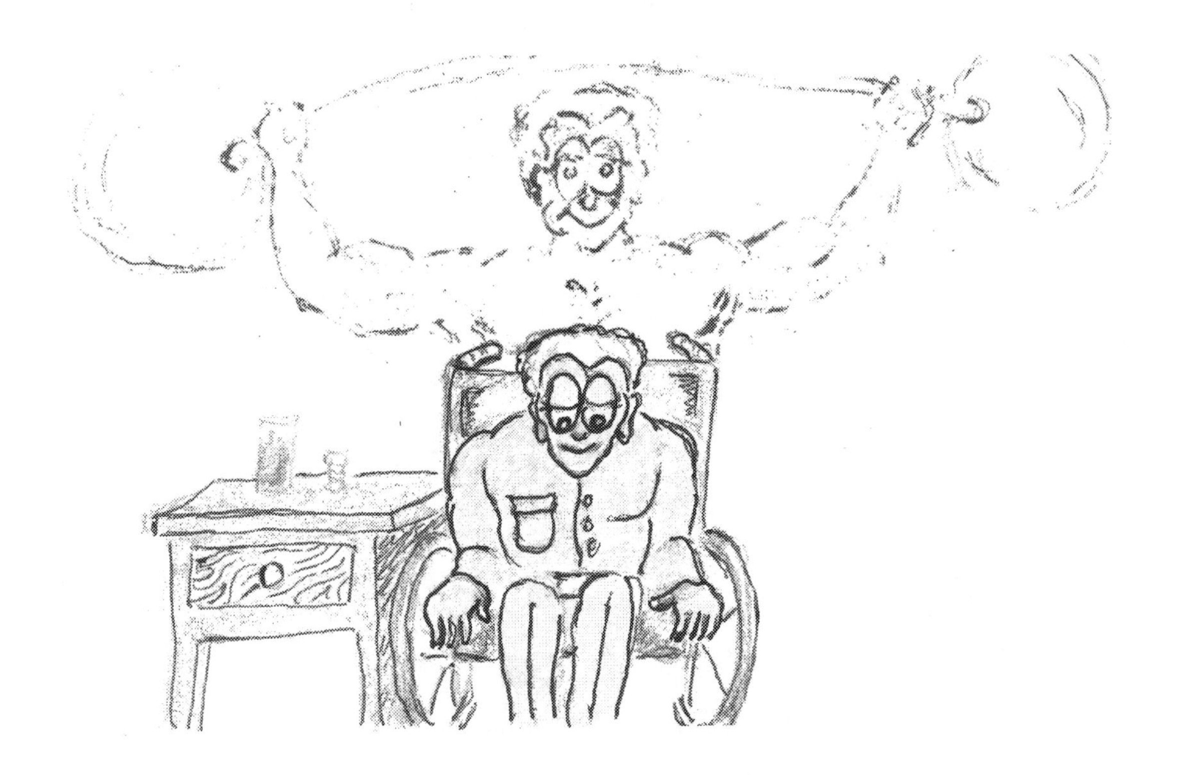

Today I exercise my excellent wheelchair-cleaning skills. I always pay dearly for this act of boldness, but it is worth it to mash the pain of the day. I learned early in this ordeal to stay as busy as possible. Even when I rest, I busy my mind so as to not give place to negative thinking. This is very important for self-preservation.

Keep your mind elevated whether sick or well. This is vital to spiritual wellness. Bodily exercise would not profit me much in this condition, so I turn to strengthening my spirit (1 Tim. 4:8). This is coming from a man who lived in a gym. I've never been this weak in body, but I've also never been this strong in spirit. My contribution to natural life is very little these days. But if you need your spirit lifted, come talk to me. I know just the man for the job.

Jesus, of course, is the ultimate example of transforming from this life to the next. In Him, I have courage to pray in a lion's den or to sing in a prison cell. I still have a great love for life but little respect for mere survival.

Another day, and it is well with my soul. Going on noon, and I'm still trying to decide what sounds good for breakfast. I need food because I can't have medicine without it. I need my pain pill, you know! I know all this sounds bad, but between Shell, me, and the Spirit of God, there is a spirit of worship in the room this morning. At this point, we are not asking God for anything. We're just praising Him for what He has already done. Our two good friends, goodness and mercy, are always present and accounted for (Ps. 23).

I'm coming to the end of this particular writing. Doing this, I'm more blessed than I could have ever imaged. Pure love is pulling things out of me that I never thought I possessed. This is where everyone in my life benefits from my presence (those who are in my life circle). I always hope that my character will be a blessing to those who get close enough to experience it.

I love when people allow you to be yourself and do not try to pull you out of your character by their actions. This is where my confidence in self through God really counts. When the enemy (Satan the accuser) comes in like a flood, God will lift up a standard—Jesus, who is not only God's Son but a way of life.

My example of pure love. My first love under God, of course. She introduced me to Jesus years ago, not knowing that He would become the only power that's keeping me alive. Her life made Christ so real to me until I now have total confidence in Him. She lived life so close to God that she had a beautiful death. A good beginning is nice, but a good ending is better. I love the way Mom turned every single battle in her life over to the Lord. I never in all the years I knew her saw anything but Christ working in her life. So I know that that same victory is in me. She was not bound in life or death. Thank you, Jesus!

When things are bad, I close my eyes and keep my pain to Jesus and to myself as much as possible. If I am in pain, I don't need everyone around me to suffer. This is God's plan concerning me. You must decide whether or not you trust Him to that extent. I'll continue to trust the God that made me over anyone else's word. In terms of God's glory, which is my whole life's design, this whole situation is but light affliction (2 Cor. 4:17). Maybe it's a Job test (Job 2:3). Being considered by God is in no way a bad thing. Trees go through storms all the time. The ones that are well watered and planted in solid ground may lose a limb, bend a little, and lose some leaves, but they always look stronger and better after the storm.

I don't feel like leaving the house, but it's Neo's second birthday. Of course, my body is objecting to the whole idea of moving today, not to mention it's a hundred degrees outside. Heat and pain don't go together. Time for a sacrifice (Rom. 12:1). Neo loves his Pawpaw, so Pawpaw will be part of his celebration. Sometimes you just have to make a good showing. You don't lose your place in life just because you're sick. It just takes a little more faith to fulfil it. So I'm sitting at this family restaurant in this hard, uncomfortable chair, eating food I don't particularly want, looking at my beautiful babies with smiling faces. I'll take those smiles and patch my wounds for the day.

Sunday morning again. My eyes open at seven o'clock. I'm feeling pressure in my midsection. However, I know I'm going to church. In what condition, I don't know. Whatever I do today is going to hurt, so I might as well make it look good. I get up to take my shower, which is a feat all of its own. It takes me forever to finish so I try to sneak in before everyone wakes up. Everything is about budgeting time and strength. Sometimes I have plenty of one and not enough of the other. Nowadays, my days must be planned. I sometimes attend two services on Sunday, but today I have strength for only one.

It's like an airplane with two engines. If one stops working in midair, they shift all power to the remaining engine in order to stay airborne. Giving up is not an option because there are passengers who need to reach their destinations. Even if it's only to see you one more day, I've learned to put all that I have into the situation that would be the most profitable in a day. Spiritual first, then natural.

Adapt and adjust. That's an old Marine Corps saying that fits in my life very well. These days, you'd be surprised the things that come back to you when failure is not an option.

I know where Hawaii got its sunshine from that day. What a wonderful smile. We were in Hawaii that day, and I was in an enormous amount of pain from the long flight. But this smile is worth a lifetime of pain. Not one place that we have ever been in life brought this much joy to my love. So I sucked it way up and let her enjoy this to the fullest, no limits. She will ever remember the beauty of this place and these wonderful saints of God on the island of Hawaii.

I will add to her experience wherever I can, but I will never subtract. At home again, she will join me in my sickness but not here. This will be a wonderful break from cancer life (notice I didn't say death). Do you see any death in that smile? I don't. I will piggyback off of her love and beauty as long as the Lord will allow me to. I want God to be glad that He trusted me with his baby girl.

Up again, and mercy is still alive in my life. The sun is shining. A radiant light that says, "Get up and do something that's full of life and love, so everyone can see it in this brilliant light." You didn't know the day could talk, did you? I'm so glad it does because my condition tries to scream over all that heavenly glory. I opened my eyes this morning, hoping that someone is writing me a check for the boxing match I was in last night that I don't quite remember. I have all this pain in my jaw. I took a good right jab that rocked my world.

Doctor Parchman warned me that if I got a toothache with these bone shots, it would be bad. I love the doctor's honesty, but I hate the manifestation. Ouch! I can usually get through the day with the over-the-counter stuff but not today. Time for the big guns. The worst possible thing to do in this situation is to sit in a corner and do nothing. In the corner is my wheelchair, and in the kitchen, there are dishes, and my wife has to work. I'll do those dishes so that her home load is lighter. At this point, I'll do whatever my hands find to do that keeps my mind off of this pain. I won't stand still and let pain beat on me. I'll fight back!

Cancer was my stop sign telling me to stop dying and go ahead and live the rest of my life. People are fascinated with zombies because sometime what we call life turns us into zombies. At this point, we deal with one another as if we have no feeling or hope and the only person that matters on earth is me (2 Tim. 3:2). I was a very strong man in my health, able to handle any situation in a single bound. Never stopping, always in motion, and just as dead as I could be.

I was dying, my marriage was dying, dead connections with the kids. But here comes cancer. Wow, can't step over that and keep going. We always do what we want to do in life, but God lets things happen so we will do what we need to do in life. For me, cancer is extreme but very effective.

All days are not peachy keen. I'm still dealing with a raging toothache that would drive me mad if I let it. Having dental work will stop the shots that keep my bone cancer at bay for three months. No fancy choices here. Let's get this thing done so that we can move forward. Fix them? Remove them? We will see.

The sun is now going down, giving way to night. Now I must focus more to take in the light that is provided for me by the Lord (Gen. 1:16). God knew we would put ourselves through these processes where we wouldn't sleep at night, so He even gave us light to see His glory in the dark. How do you top that kind of love?

Things like that (night light) is why I find it hard to complain. If we lived the lives that we were designed to live, we would not have found ourselves in darkness. We would have been forever in the light of God's glory. But look at our loving Father who put some of Himself in that darkness because He knew that eventually we would find ourselves staring into that darkness or standing smack-dab in the middle of it. Our choices.

I never drank or smoked, but I didn't eat right and haven't always done the right thing either. This is what mapped my path in life. If you keep your vehicle in good repair and on the right highway, it will perform at the top of its ability. Let's just say I've missed the mark a few times. But God! Conditions are not always ideal, but don't give up before you even start. I got some things done today even in this condition. Start from where you are.

Those who love you always accept the best you can do, so do your best. I love life. I seek it in every situation. This means I must keep moving in a positive direction. As long as I can generate love for others and for myself, life will continue day by day. So I end this day with much hope for tomorrow.

Good Lord, where do I start today? At the beginning, I guess. Today, I don't just open my eyes. I just peek to see what the day looks like. My feelings don't match what I see. I see beautiful sunlight coming through the windows. My soul is blessed at just the sight of such a God-given day, but my face is in great pain. I must get this tooth out now. So my day starts at a dentist's office with a back tooth being drilled out of my head. I put on my game face over the top of my pain face so that I can properly deal with this soul that God made without any excessive pain reaction (I might have just made that up). Going through this whole ordeal, I'm being pain trained by the Spirit. They say wounded dogs will strike, but I'm not a dog. Neither do I strike.

So, you see, even this is a day that the Lord has made. Since this is His day, I will seek His purpose for me still being here. Not much I can do under the influence of so much pain and medicine. Near the end of the day, in walk my grandbabies. They don't know anything about bad teeth, medicine, or debilitating pain. All they know is Pawpaw's love, smiles, hugs, and treats. So here I go again. Pain has to wait until I'm done spoiling them for the day. God, give me strength! The start was rough. I need a strong finish.

This morning is a stormy one. We have lightning and thunder and plenty of sweeping rain. Today is my most painful doctor's appointment. I know it's coming every six weeks, but there is no way to prepare for it. Bad day, huh? Call me crazy, but God's glory even wins today. I happen to love thunderstorms and the fresh smell of rain. That makes the sliding doors in our bedroom nice. Once the curtains are pulled back, I have an instant weather report. I've always thought of lightning as God's natural power, as it is uncontrolled power that can't be harnessed. It's just like His spiritual power that He harnessed in the fleshly body of Jesus Christ (Mark 4:39). I don't expect everyone to believe as I do, but I know that this account in the Bible happened because still today cancer is a complete storm. People with cancer know that it storms at times, and the dryland seems unreachable. Just a simple word or phrase from God or from His Word speaks peace into my situation, and I'm functional once more.

I'm blessed because there are people who are perfectly healthy that are very dysfunctional. My physicians are a great blessing, and I don't need a mental health doctor. God's Spirit keeps me in perfect peace through unpredictable changes (John 16:20–30). In every phase of life, how you see things (your perception) is filtered by who you know. I know the Creator, so this storm is not a disaster; it's awesome power!

Saturday morning, and God has blessed me with a medium pain level, and I'm very grateful. I'm looking for something to do outside of the house. At the same time, I'm playing it by ear because I don't know how tired my hardworking wife is. Remember, I can't work anymore, so these days I'm just a trophy husband (LOL). I don't consider myself dying, just living life with cancer. We live with a lot of undesirable things; mine is just cancer.

Looks like a visit to my mother-in-law's house. That's not a bad thing. I love my mother-in-law. If I had to describe her to you, I would say watch the movie *War Room*. She reminds me a lot of that wonderful spiritual lady with all that good wisdom. I love to take my wife to her mom's house. Of the three wonderful daughters my mother-in-law had, my wife is the only one who still lives in town, and they are very close. I took her away from her mom as a young man, but I have also had the joy of bringing her back as the first son-in-law. Of course, the in-law part has long ago dropped off, and now I'm just plain son. The timing couldn't be better, as my birth mom went on to be with the Lord years ago. I went from a ratty old high school boyfriend to a son-in-law to just plain son. I love it, but, gentlemen, you have to earn it.

I'm up early Sunday morning at six o'clock. The room is filled with the sound of the TV reading the King James Version of the Bible. The words of life. I believe in starting my day with life. The process of a day has its way of draining life out of you. It's just like fueling any other engine. In order for it to run, you must put something in the fuel tank. The better the fuel, the better the performance. I'm good to go this morning. I'm ready to share some of this positive energy from this morning's fueling session.

Through the filter of God's Word that I'm hearing through the TV, the rain is a gentle rain that is transformed from water drops to drops of love from heaven to wash clean my way for a visit with my heavenly Father on His day of visitation. I will enjoy it.

Getting to church was everything I hoped it would be. The Spirit of God just worked around those who weren't in the mood for church and proceeded to bless those of us who were in the mood. I actually had enough energy to sing a song with my Shell. That alone was a blessing and a lifter of my head. Being caught up in something so positive, all negativity must remain on standby, at least until you come down from that spiritual high.

I'm not a man of means anymore. I haven't worked in a couple of years now. My doctor bills take most of what I get, but I want to accumulate something for my little ones to enjoy. So as broke as Pawpaw is, the bank of Pawpaw and Mawmaw still exists. We are blessed to go and do as we please. How, you ask? When you figure it out, let me know. I know it's not money; it's God's favor. I will work harder for God's favor than I've ever worked for any dollar bill.

I can't begin to tell you what I have done or where I have been, because if I do, I just might get audited by the IRS, and I have no answers except God is good.

Shell and I have this little system where after we pay our obligations and bills and feed ourselves, any money left over is turned into coins. It's funny how it works out. When the coin jars fill up, it's usually the same time one of the kids needs money. We never have to tell them no. They just have to roll up some coins. The whole system seems to work smoothly. God's favor includes knowledge on how to handle what you have, whether it's millions or two fish and five loaves of bread (Matt. 14:17–20). So, you see, it's not what you have. It's who you know. Training myself with coins has curved my spending desires drastically. I'm not going to roll up coins to buy something I don't need.

This is where I get my art skills from, Mathue Jo'el, better known as Big Mac. His uncle Dave would say "with the cheese." He's my youngest, insanely talented son. He and his wife, Vicky, single-handedly blessed the world with Nic, Neo, and Brini girl. In tough situations, it always helps to have something good to live for, especially in a world that only broadcasts mass destruction. Mat will put some graphics on Facebook or drop by with my babies, and suddenly the day has true meaning again. Sometimes it seems like me and Shell against the world, but these guys always remind us that we have an excellent home team. Go team! Always a winning experience when we're together. When the time comes for me to move on, my family will be fine. I have three men that will take my place and do a better job than I did. Thank you, Myke, Mat, and Corey.

Watching a movie called *Dead Man Walking*. Interesting choice for someone like me. A movie about a man on death row. This guy goes through the whole movie knowing that he was guilty of murder and would soon face death. But he gambled with a lawyer to keep the truth from surfacing and possibly getting away with it.

This is not what happens at all. The truth, being ordained by God Himself, will always come to the surface. Either you can repent, which means to confess and turn away from your wrongdoing and warn others of the traps that you yourself fell into, or you can hide it and watch lives be destroyed the same way yours was.

It is a very good thing when your mistakes become a teaching opportunity that helps someone else. If my life is the beginning of a nasty domino effect disaster, that's not a good thing. In life and in death, we all stand beside God's Son, Jesus, who God fully approved of, being Father and Creator. In life, we do our best to gain the approval of the Father because His remembrance of our life is our ticket to paradise, both now and later (Luke 23:42).

Thursday will be fun. I have scans all day starting at 9:45 a.m. The first one is a CAT scan. I told them we have two to choose from. One gray with a bad attitude and hairy, and the other, gray striped, layered female. They choose me instead. Lucky me (LOL). Next, there's the bone scan. Can't have too many of those now, can I? I guess they need to see how aggressive this terror called cancer is in my bones and so forth.

Just like any other terrorist, a threat can be handled and disposed of. I won't be held hostage by a threat. Whatever results these scans produce are all covered in my life insurance plan. I guess I should worry, huh? Worrying puts you in a bad place and makes you hard to deal with. I worry more about being offensive than being sick. It's all about seeing how well you perform under pressure. It's the golden rule (Matt. 7:12). I totally expect cancer to act like cancer, but I also expect to act like a man (God's man). So through the shots and time-consuming discomfort, I will be me and not who cancer wants me to be. I know it doesn't bother some people, but I'm not comfortable being out of character. I will have my scans tomorrow and go on living with the results. If good, we sail through fair weather; if not, we sail the rough seas. Either way, we sail.

I actually thought I had a peaceful night ahead. I was set to rest and get ready for tomorrow, but that peace was disturbed by yelling and police lights outside my window. *That's fine. Things happen,* I thought. *We don't live in a perfect world.* This thinking is reasonable until I find out what's actually happening.

Some old enemies of my granddaughters decided tonight was a good night to come across town, onto my property, to start a fight with my granddaughters. Real classy move. These kids were brought over to this side of town (get this) by their mother and grandmother, who will now be arrested for it. All of this because my granddaughter didn't like one the girl's brother. It amazes me that any adult would be involved in such childish matters. I would not dream of stepping down from my fatherhood to become a spoiled little child again. My condition does not allow me to go backward, only forward. I know these situations are designed to drag you down to a dark, negative place that sickness and hate can feed off of. I have no time or space for this in what's left of my life.

Between God, the proper authorities, and my granddaughter's parents, I will remain a figure of steadfast love for my girls and their parents.

I'm scanning this morning. This requires blood tests and needles and delicious cocktails of radioactive juices put into my veins so that my bones can be photographed by machines. They don't use IVs on me anymore. I have a power port. This means they no longer have to hunt down a vein to inject or take blood. They just go to the port in my chest.

Now the second half of the bone scan. The first scan was fifteen minutes. The second scan was fifty minutes flat on my back, being perfectly still on a hard table, which made it seem like hours. This is important for good pictures. No do-overs please! A full day of doctors and hospital visits. Not exactly painful, just annoying. In this phase of life, that's normal. Don't get me wrong. I really appreciate the great patchwork my doctors do on this jacked-up, old junk pile of a body.

With this wonderful technology we have today, you can actually find out how many of your classmates are still alive. Some of the most popular and healthy of my classmates died at early ages. I'm thinking, *Boy, I'm living on borrowed time, and I'm extremely blessed.* I will gladly suffer these minor inconveniences and live a little longer for my loved ones.

This is Marea J. Benford, my baby girl and spiritual twin. She laughs when I laugh and cries when I cry and even feels my pain. She, like her daddy, is a preacher sent from God. The sooner she realizes this, the more peace she'll have. The object of Daddy's love. For what I am going through, her presence is required. I must feel the spirit of my only baby girl in the house. Every father should have at least one spoiled daddy's girl for these times in life.

If you don't have one, get one for your own sake. They are among God's greatest blessings and great spiritual medicine for whatever it is that troubles you. This rascal keeps me smiling.

I wasn't worried about all the scans on Thursday, although a bit curious. I will learn to totally trust God, as I should this time. I was thinking during the night, wondering what the scans would show. Is the cancer moving? Is it worse? These things came to mind, and in the past, I had a bad habit of preparing myself for the worst. No reason for all of that. The scan information was great. God has blessed the skills of my doctors to keep this stuff at bay with treatment and medicine.

This is the benefit of service to a loving God, and He loves me. This kind of favor is worth more than anything this world could ever afford. Cancer is there, but it doesn't have permission from God to do anything until He says so. Like Judas, he was with Jesus through His whole ministry. He was a part of the ministry. He was chosen by God to be a part of it, and look at his purpose and reason for being there. However, even in all of this, Judas could not have his move until Jesus released him (John 13:27). Guess what? Cancer is subject to God's release also. My scans show that God has not released cancer to take my body, so I yet abide in His wonderful mercy. Humans tell me this is stage 4; God says, "Hold your peace."

I was blessed to have a full weekend, so busy that I forgot to take my medicine (don't tell my docs). Being surrounded by all of my family both Saturday and Sunday was wonderful. True Christmas in July. All the pretty babies I could stand. Church service was a blessing. God spoke from His throne to a speck of dust like me. Every Word He speaks improves my life. I sat on hard, uncomfortable chairs and benches all day and didn't mind it because God's Word is so uplifting.

Saturday contained two emotional events. A memorial dinner in honor of my daughter-in-law's (Teenie) sister and my father-in-law, Big Daddy Sims, moving out of the house he built from the ground up to a senior facility. Both sad but needful, so I'll be there for support for both. For Teenie, it was the person she loved most dearly. Big Daddy had to leave everything he worked for and move in with people he doesn't know. His estate was no small matter, so this situation is not exactly an ego booster.

The presence of godly people makes all the difference because they breed hope in situations where there seems to be no hope.

Mykal Joe is my oldest son, one of the greatest sons on earth, honored by his father and rightly so. If life cuts me down, I will be stronger than ever in this man. Proven in my weakest hour, he stood for me when I could not stand. There is your son of perfection. Educated and successful yet humble with a measure of wisdom. What a winning mix. He brought me back to life with constant care and love fit for a king. Today, as I sit and draw this picture, that whole experience floods back to my mind. As his father, I am humbled by his actions. The easy thing would have been a long, horrible nursing home stay with visits every now and them, but that didn't happen because of him and Teenie.

There is indeed a wonderful table prepared by the Lord Jesus Christ that sits right in the very presence of my enemy (Ps. 23:5), which in my case reveals itself as cancer. On this table today is much encouragement, much joy, and much peace. I don't know about the rest of this world, but I am encouraged by my place in Christ. This was reinforced by a preacher who let God speak through him without being in self. In a way, it's like electricity flowing directly from the source with no filter or transmitters. We know that this sort of power is known as lightning, natural power from heaven.

I'm not stumbling through this valley or crawling. I have not been brought to my knees by this enemy. But because of God's Word, I am walking upright through this valley of death, trying to project the light of the Holy Ghost, which causes death to remain just a shadow that is not relevant in my life. What a great thing, to be chosen and resting and feasting at the Lord's Table.

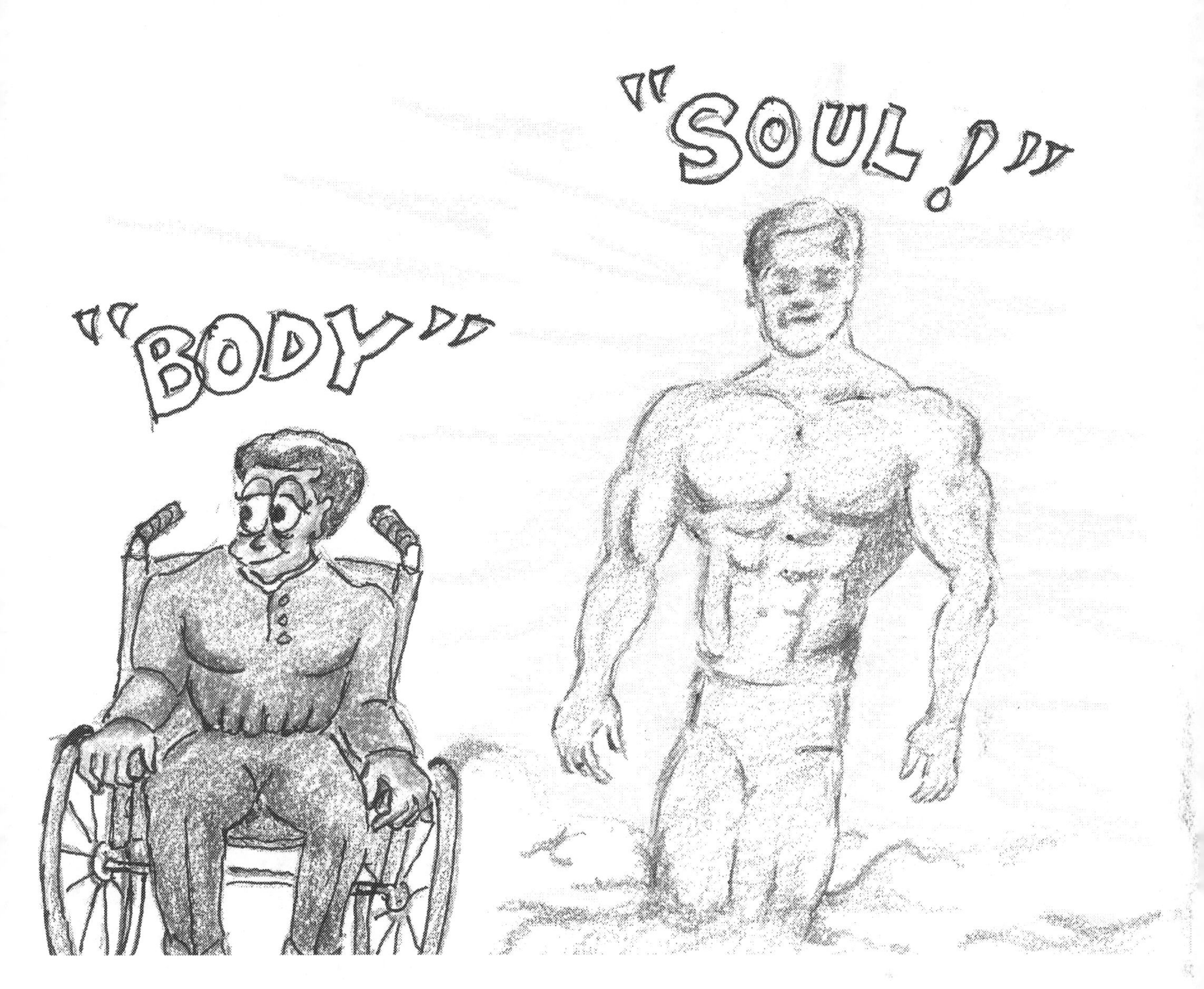

The body is not so great, but look at that soul. I can't visit the gym anymore, but look at what God's Word has done to my soul. When I was strong naturally, I was weak spiritually. I'm not saying this as a blanket statement. There are some who have the blessing of balance, not me. I was either taking care of business or feeding my soul, never both together. When sickness caused me to flip the script, oh what a blessing I found. The Lord has blessed me with a desire for more of Him, and it's been a soul food buffet. I spend lots of time focusing on God's Word. What a world of great wonder, and it all applies to me and my benefit package in Christ. I sing simply because I'm happy. I sing simply because I'm free. God's eye is on the sparrow, and I know He watches me.

My favorite movie personality is Arnold Schwarzenegger. I wonder if his soul looks anything like his body. Is he able to save a nation with his strength like Samson? I really love having a strong soul, because anything the body gets me into, the soul (being the dwelling place of my portion of God's Spirit) can get me out of simply by believing and trusting God.

I don't really concern myself with sin these days. To sin is to take out a loan against your own life that you can never pay back. This is absolute foolishness. I don't willingly sin, but if I unknowingly do, I'm glad God's grace is completely sufficient for me.

I'm sitting here looking at the cruise ship that the Lord has blessed me and Shell to cruise on in just a few days. Our boat is the *Emerald*, part of the Princess line. This is premium cruising, not bad for our income. With a few payments and a lot of heavenly favor, here we go again—and not a minute too soon. My Shell is getting frustrated with her job and life in general. The general part could very well be her constant care of me. While we're on this vacation, I'll have to come up with ways to lighten her load.

She'll say something like, "Babe, you're not a burden," but with all the stuff that's wrong with me, my eyes work very well. It's hard to watch someone I love so dearly stress out. Believe me, love will find a way to lighten her load so that her wonderful smile will stay put. My favorite chair sits right next to her workstation, and I watch as she interacts with people under so much pressure. Flawless in character, she is.

I know the stress symptoms and look because my job was stressful. All those super Christians who say, "I'm too blessed to be stressed" have not read or understood the Beatitudes (Matt. 5:1–12). Blessings come with stress most of the time. This is Christ's definition of being blessed. So where are your blessings coming from?

Just days before vacation, and I can't seem to get any energy from any source. I want to get up and do something, anything, but it seems like there is a giant hand pushing me back into my chair. This feeling gets greater the more my sugar numbers go down. I guess my body is not used to being that low in sugar. I lost so much muscle mass in my first hospital stay, and I still haven't gained a fraction of it back. With Mr. Catheter limiting my movements, exercise is at a cardiac level and not muscle building. What's really crazy is some of my meds make me gain weight but not muscle. So I have extra fat on weak legs. Talk about out of balance.

Nevertheless, God is still good, and my life is extremely blessed. I have a wheelchair and a scooter to carry me from place to place, so I'm still able to participate in the life of my family, and I don't miss much. I have a really good excuse to avoid those situations that I don't want to be involved with. Life could be worse.

I would really like some energy from somewhere. I have days when the Spirit is willing, but the flesh is weak.

I'm sure this vacation will breathe new life into our situation, granting us a new grip on life. As part of the true vine, we continue to blossom into new life again and again (John 15:1).

All this talk about cancer. I hate the idea of this nasty stuff, but I love the fact that this sickness made a way for life. Simple life. People need to master the art of downsizing. We live in a society where more is always better. That is a textbook example of addiction. We have a whole society that's addicted to stuff. My life is so simple. I can breathe now, and it feels really good. If I had this kind of sense when I was working, every corner of my house would be full of money.

Shell and I got married at nineteen. Our kids have been grown and on their own since we were forty. We've had fifteen years of working with no dependents. We were too busy working to save or live. Funny how life works. Working people retire in one or two ways. Either you retire when you're seventy-two and only have a few years left to leave everything you worked for to someone else, praying that they will do something good with it, or your body is so broken down you can't really enjoy it because of aches and pains. You can't really enjoy it while you're working because you spend all your time on the job. Overtime? Your money doubles, and your days disappear like vapor. You have no idea where the time went. Minutes turn into hours, hours turn into days, days turn into months, and months turn into years. Now you're old, and nothing really matters but a day without pain. Try to get something good out of every day.

What I really like about an excellent spirit is that it comes from God. This is a spirit of love. Because of religion, people don't realize that it's just that simple. This is the thing I don't like about religious stuff. It tends to take the wonderful simplicity of the Gospel of Jesus Christ and complicate it for all sorts of reasons, mostly fear and personal gain.

No sane person can understand the work that Jesus did to free us from sin and then continue to sin against themselves and God. Once you understand salvation, you won't continue to sin. As a preacher myself, I am here to help you understand John 3:16. God said, if you believe and accept Jesus's work on the cross, you don't have to perish. So I simply told myself, "I believe, and I won't perish." Believing caused me to turn away from sin and soul destruction.

I understand the safety of Christ because He is pure love. No sin or darkness of any kind. I understand that in a field of pure love, no darkness of any kind can grow. To dwell in the midst of love is to always be in brilliant light. I'm so glad my family loves me. It's bad when families don't have a strong foundation of love. If you notice anything that needs to be held together, permanent love is the best glue.

My choices today are family reunion or funeral. Reunion on the Hodge side, funeral on the Kidd side. It's a beautiful day to do anything. My energy level is a bit low, so I do nothing. I guess I'll have some breakfast and see if that raises my levels a little. I'm not complaining by any means. I just have desires. I'm believing God for energy to get something done around the house this weekend. Sitting out in the hot sun on a hard wooden beach will not work for me right now. Not to mention the wonderful bug population you have to fight just to eat a sandwich in peace. The aftermath of sitting out there will punish me severely.

If I were well, I'd definitely be at the funeral because that's what we do. We go and listen to a preacher put a person in heaven even though they didn't follow any of God's rules. Would you let someone in your house that hates you and doesn't follow any of your rules? That's not going to happen. How do we believe that God is going to pump all his rules and let us in heaven to pollute purity with sin? We get an invitation to heaven all our lives. It's not God's fault if we throw them in the trash can next to our desk (Matt. 11:23). A preacher who knows nothing about that person's life tells everyone in the room they're in God's house now, trying to force them into heaven even though they turned it away all their life.

It doesn't do me a lot of good to visit churches where the pastor preaches sin and sin only all the time. In my present state, I know about sin and have been in, around, and through sin. But in all of this, I never really understood the root of sin. Sin is not just cheating on your spouse or drinking, smoking, or even fighting; it is anything that draws you away from God and makes you forget who He is.

I might have said this before, but some people stop doing things simply because they get too old to do them anymore. That does not make you any closer to God. Old age and sickness are not good reasons to seek God. To understand who He is and love Him for who He is—that is the key to a well-balanced soul.

Not that I understand a fraction of who God is. I love Him to the point that sin is my worst enemy. I will flee it at all costs. This is to please God and remain in His favor. Favor? Then why do you have cancer? My friend, God is not handing out cancer. Bad eating, bad air, or bad water could be the cause for all we know. God didn't caused any of this. Favor because this stuff is eating away at me, but it can't take me until God says so. It can't pain me, cripple me, or stop me because I have God's favor. Satan can only operate outside of the hedge (Job 1:10).

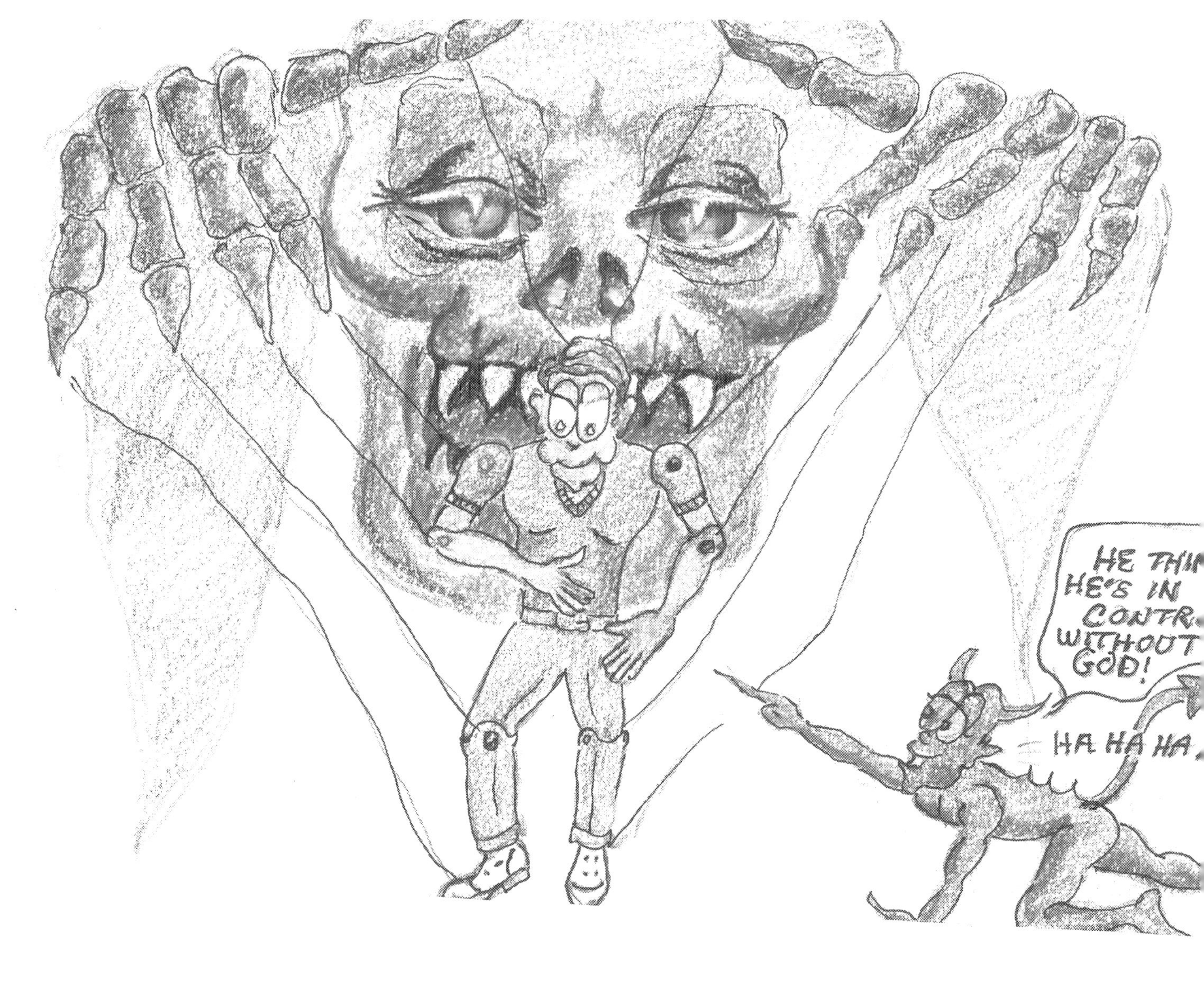

This life hinges on appearances. I know the difference between a God that's real and one that simply sets a stage. On this stage of life, depending on who you believe in, things can get out of sorts. Who's behind the scene? Who's pulling the strings? Face the facts. Flesh is dust (Gen. 2:7). Something is moving you, right or wrong, good or bad.

Life is full of situations and problems that are all magnified by appearances. God's Word is settled in heaven. In His Word, there's no room for problems to grow or get out of hand. Nothing surprises God. Is there anything too hard for God? I don't think so. Satan has never been a roaring lion, only *as* a roaring lion. He is not a god but a rejected angel. This is one of those things that causes me to kick myself—the fact that I let him talk me into damaging myself and only for fleeting pleasures. Everything in life appears so wonderful as long as you're being self-centered and it doesn't bring any glory to God.

So many things in life wear intricate disguises. If we don't pay very close attention, we'll never see them. Satan rambles around in our emotions, trying to make us think we're spiritual. When being emotional, our good intentions don't last until we get outside of the church doors. We must love God. When we love God, we love everything He created. This kind of gets rid of the hate problem, huh?

It's hard to believe how easy people fall for stuff we call the dream life. This is a lifestyle that pulls us in so many different directions that we sometimes live in a constant state of confusion. Some of our madness is organized, and some is unorganized. As long as Satan can keep humankind unbalanced, his work is very easy and undetectable (Luke 22:31). In this scripture, Jesus talks about a sifting. This is to separate. People are divided in everything these days. Is this a successful sifting?

Jesus said, "I'll make you fishers of men" (Matt 4:19). Ever notice how Satan reversed that? Humankind gets hoodwinked on so many things it's unreal. Speaking of unreal, if you know anything about the sport of angling, then you know that the bass fish is the top of the food chain. In many aspects, humankind is just like the mighty bass fish. There is a largemouth bass and a smallmouth bass. They seldom strike real bait. Just like humankind, if it's shiny and has great moves, you will catch your limit in no time. There is excitement with catching and releasing them. You can catch the same fish two or three times in the same trip with the same bait. One day that fish will run out of luck and meet the angler who wants a fish dinner, and that bass will never see that lake again. It's all because of fake bait.

This morning, I happened to look at Facebook, and someone said church is the last functional institution of slavery still in service. I will give you that to a degree, but what does that have to do with mine or your walk with God? It's called misrepresentation. Many churches under or misrepresent God because of ignorance or greed or they are just plain evil.

Out of all the religions that existed in Jesus's time, we don't find Jesus a member of any. Yet He was the only way approved by God (Matt 3:17) (John 14: 6). In this case, don't focus on the man Jesus but focus on the way. His color and nationality don't matter, just the fact that His character and life pleased the God of heaven. The same heaven everyone wants to go to.

You can do whatever you're old enough to do in a church, but in *the way*, there is only holiness (Is. 35:8), and this is built upon that rock (Jesus) (Dan. 2:45). Jesus said, "I build my church." This means His following (Matt. 16:18). He wasn't talking about Peter because, like many of us, Peter's ability to follow was limited and in the natural only. We see when things got spiritual, Peter had to deny Him even after being warned by Jesus. This is why we need the power of the Holy Ghost: because only a Spirit, which is Jesus Christ, can walk in God's way. You don't get the Holy Ghost from a church but from God.

I do understand how and why people feel so bound. This generation is all about mind clutter. They have something blocking all their natural senses. On their head, they have headphones constantly pumping foul music through their brain, completely controlling their thought process and poisoning the thoughts they form. Yet they're free?

Before their eyes, they have a cell phone with the internet. On it, all the filth you can ever imagine. If you can imagine it, it's on there. Remember what God said about humankind's imagination (Gen. 6:5). What a wonderful way to cultivate kids, huh? Just release them into a world of technology and terror and walk away. Freedom, huh?

In their hand, everything they can imagine to use however they please, with no instruction or experience. They have the equivalence of an atom bomb to use as firecrackers, totally destroying their lives before they get started. But they're free. Their emotions totally and completely run their lives because they have no sense of reality. This renders them socially dysfunctional. They really just don't get along with one another.

They don't eat anything that doesn't taste good, no matter if it keeps you healthy or not. They eat stuff that the human body can't process, but they still think they're free.

My life is hidden in Christ. Where He is, so am I. I don't have to worry about all these things. I am free to walk in heavenly places even on earth. Fleshly desires will never allow you to be free. Satan offered Adam and Eve freedom in the garden, and their choice put chains on all humankind. To be without God doesn't put you in control; it leaves you out of control.

For many years, my mind had been poisoned by religious sayings and clichés such as "you need God *in your life*." This is to say, my life is still controlled by me; I just need God when I run into trouble. This creates a false sense of stability in life and salvation. This kind of thinking makes God not only very small but also effective and real only in small part of our lives. So, like many people, I had brought the King of Glory down to waiting tables in my life and getting mad when he didn't do what I asked Him to do.

Too blessed to be stressed is not when all your bills are paid, you're driving the car you want, and you live in the house of your dreams. Too blessed to be stressed is when none of this stuff matters, or you have nothing but God and a heart and mind to glorify Him in all that you do. As far as God waiting your table for you, do you call the president when you have car trouble? Nope, you don't.

I have way more faith in my heavenly Father than any earthly authority. He knows my situation and is doing what best glorifies Him in me. I'm good with that. Yes, I am blessed.

Sunday morning, and my natural man doesn't even feel like putting clothes on, but I know it's time for me to put God on His throne in my life. This opportunity alone motivates me to get up, get clothes, and walk victoriously through the day in Jesus's name. My suffering is a small price to pay to live in such glory. For me, this is what it takes to drop the fig leaves and still be totally covered (Gen. 3:7).

Through all of this God, allows me to see His purpose over the horror of the situation. There's something about human arrogance that, if God allows us to live through more than one hurricane, to us it becomes an average storm. This is because they see some of what's happening, but they can't see all that God would not let happen (Job 1:10).

So, why is life so painful at times? How mad would you be if you were the prince of powers (Eph. 2:2) and your verdict for my life was death, and along comes Jesus and overrules your verdict? You would be an angry prince. You're going to do all you can to make me uncomfortable. So, needless to say, I'm not hung up on comfort or justice in this life, only what's right in the sight of God. People get really hung up on their rights these days, but the rights of a Christian is to be Christ-like. We are not of this world.

Saturday, time to enjoy a day with my wife and mother-in-law. I have a feeling this is not going to be a regular day. I was right. Showering, getting dressed, charging my wheelchair and getting it ready was fun enough. Simple, right? We get to Mom's house, I get out of the car to switch seats with my wife, and down I go. I hit the ground hard. In my condition, you feel this on so many painful levels.

Now I lie here plotting a strategy of how to get up without showing too much pain. I don't want to ruin the day. You learn to take one for the team every once in a while. That's a good thing. You learn to put things that don't matter to the back of your mind and go on with your life. I'm so glad I did because the rest of the day was pretty nice.

We saw a very nice play that was so skillfully done it would have been a shame to miss it or not enjoy it. I've learned to enjoy the good in life. I seek only the good and let the bad catch me wherever it can.

I consume as much of my family's life as they will allow me to without being in the way. I know they have their own lives too. So, as long as my situation is manageable, I'll manage it and move on.

What a difference a day makes. Yesterday was not exactly a high point in my life, but today I'm king of the Danish. Let me explain. This is an English assignment of my oldest grandchild, Kymmie. A production of *Beowulf King of the Geeks*. Yes, geeks. I was king of the Danish. This lofty position comes complete with cardboard shoulder pads and a crown made of an apple Danish. In case you haven't figured it out yet, there's some fancy grandpa'ing (my new word) going on here. Yes, granddaughters can talk grandpas into anything. So here I am with Danish on my head, looking like a fourteen-carat nut. But she will get a good grade in English. Everyone had a great time filming this major motion picture on cell phones at night, in the park, with giant mosquitos consuming our flesh.

I enjoy watching more and more of myself disappear and someone more Godlike taking my place. He's more patient, kind, and loving toward others. He seeks out the satisfactions of others. So, I ask you, cancer tragedy or wake-up call? What do you think?

I wonder if I would have seen the importance of participating in this production had I been healthy and working every hour of the day to gain more money and stuff. I find that my situation makes me available to good works.

I went to a funeral today. Looking down on the body of a friend who died of the same cancer I'm living with. God begins to make me aware of the purpose of my body. It is to carry His divine Spirit and to act out light in a dark world (Matt. 5:14). I hate to use the term death, but that's the term people understand.

I looked on this brother's body, dressed in his finest suit with a nice haircut, looking ten years younger. I can tell that because of his trust in God he has continued on to that prepared place that Christ went to make for those who love Him (John 14:2). It's like a friend that moved from Ohio to Hawaii. You can't wait to visit him in paradise.

We were created into the family of God by God, giving us His image and dominion over all the kingdoms of this earth. Until this day, it's still our choice whether we want to continue to be the black sheep of the family. Once I realized who God is and who He made me to be, I will never again live a day outside of His glory and wonderful favor. No sickness, riches, or trial will separate me from the image of my heavenly Father. I was created to show the whole world around (Rom. 8:35).

Pleasure over purpose. It takes us too many wasted years to realize the true value of our God-given vessels—the body. So, for many years, we misuse and abuse it. By the time we understand what's going on, the damage is done. We go through most of our lives not realizing we have a purpose beyond what we see on the different media that only cater to these destructive pleasures of our flesh. No TV shows remind you that you are divinely made for a divine purpose. What great freedom you have when finally you realize that this is what has been missing in your life to bring you back in balance. Cancer happened. Leaning to one side too long causes uneven wear. I stayed away from God too long.

There are many things in life that cause this unhealthy lean. I was born into a big family that didn't have money, and I was a middle child, very easily overlooked and forgotten at times. So once I got old enough to make money (1 Tim. 6:10) and do what I wanted to do, imagine my rampage. Boy, the dark clouds that came with this mind-set. My cancer slowed me down and allowed me to see my life from my Creator's point of view. I had to get back to purpose and not so much pleasure. Pleasure is a cover for addiction, and purpose is a plan for freedom (Gal. 5:1).

In God's eyes, every single person is responsible for leading the world into a godly wisdom (Gen. 1:28). God's purpose for humankind never changed. Our willingness to do it did. Humankind was fashioned to be the gods of earth. No one above us. We live beneath our purpose, and therefore, we have no dominion. We are the crown of all creation. We often live like the scum of the earth. We are blessed to have a loving Creator that doesn't give up on us (John 3:16). As Jesus was the light of the world, we are supposed to light up every situation in our lives. Being fashioned in a way to obtain the knowledge of God, we should live according to that godly knowledge, which is everlasting light.

Have I been a leader of life and wisdom to the portion of this world that God blessed me with? Am I finally coming into balance with God's purpose because cancer has put me back in my place? I don't feel sorry for myself. I feel ashamed that it took all of this for me to realize my true purpose. It doesn't take a lion most of his life to figure out that he's a lion. Humankind still hasn't figured out how to be divine in flesh. The big clue is Jesus. God created me for Himself. I don't think any sickness will ever stop His purpose.

The thing you must ask yourself is, what am I entrusted with and how will I lead and offer up those things and people to the God that I know is Lord and Master of all? God is trusting me with His children and the wonderful woman I call my wife, and also all those whom I interact with daily. I am a steward of the Master's goods, not an owner. Instead of thinking about my life being shortened or how bad things are now that I have cancer, I must concentrate on completing life correctly, and the only correct way is God's way.

I actually really enjoy when something falls into place in my life. Since my situation, it happens more and more because self is not in the way. I feel closer to what God made me to be than ever before in life.

There is a natural display of light and also a spiritual display of lights. The natural display, God put in place from the beginning of time. Sun by day, moon and stars by night. Now there is us. We choose when and where to display our light. This light is the God in us, not just good deeds. You find a lot of bad people doing good things for personal reasons, not for the glory of God. Light can be just a display or a way of life (John 1:4).

Even those who don't view life so closely like to display light at different times to bring glory to a situation or day. Of course, I'm thinking about Christmas, which is celebrated in the darkest, coldest time of the year. It doesn't matter how broke we are or what the situation is, we go all out to make sure everyone is safe, warm, and happy during the holidays. Just like Christmas and its season, I'm in what many see as a dark, cold season of life, so my light display is in full effect. You must slow down when you drive past my house and enjoy the beauty of my light display. At the end of this dark season, you end up with all of the wonderful gifts that you asked for (John 16:23).

I guess I'm getting a little deeper because this writing is coming to an end. But I need you to understand this whole cancer life and death thing. Cancer is something that happens to a body, not a spirit. The body is a vessel; you are a spirit. Do not let your body control who you are. Strive to achieve an excellent spirit (Dan. 6:3). This will bring your body under subjection, along with its sickness and cancers, and afford you everlasting life. Do not give this negativity victory over your life and definitely not over your transformation from this life to your heavenly life.

At some point in life, we must learn to live in the glory of God that we were purposed to live in. Cancer is a tragic end to a person. Good thing I was not created to reflect humans' thoughts but to imitate a victorious, ever-living, always-loving, almighty God. Amen!

I will end this writing with lots of love for family and friends who laugh, live, and love with me every day. Praise be to God we still have some time left. I'm dealing with this every day, but I'm not in a hurry to leave my people. God knows my heart. I do so enjoy giving to them what God gives to me, lots of pure love and old-folk wisdom. Funny, huh? If you seek God and His perfect will for you, you will impart wisdom you didn't know you had.

I don't expect everyone to understand me or my point of view, but those who are in my condition will understand. Some people completely stop living when they hear "cancer." Some take on a holding pattern. Me? I took on a form of accelerated living. I'm completing things now that in my health I would have never thought of. I guess it's a thing of putting your flesh out of the way so that your spirit (the real you) can go to work. Of course, that's the way life is supposed to work anyway. Feels pretty good to have a sense of balance. Hopefully, through my experience, someone will reach that balance before they get to this point in life. Much love to all who read this!

About the Author

Joseph Hodge is a man with a high school education and 58 years of life training, experience and a measure of common sense. He was a football player during his high school years and married his high school sweetheart. They have a wonderful family and enjoy many fine things in life because of God's favor.

As a young man, he enjoyed working and earning a fair wage in the Marble and Tile Setting trade for 15 years with his life-time friend and fellow football player, Walt Davis.

He drove for Brinks Inc. prior to learning of his illness which subsequently ended his working career. He decided then to retire and spend the rest of his time with his family.

Printed in the United States
By Bookmasters